Against All Odds
(I Survived)

1. Copyright Page :

Against All Odds.. I Survived!

Published By SpiffingCovers.co.uk

ISBN no: 978-1-909425-20-0

Published April 2013

Copyright © Fikelephi Jackson 2013

Dedication: I dedicate this book to the following:

My late daughter Patience M Ncube who died at 22 years of age. To my supportive husband and my wonderful children. To Betty Makoni's mother, (Mrs. Rudo Fiona Nenguwo) who died through domestic violence. And finally to all the all the survivors.

Acknowledgement

Firstly I thank God for the opportunity to share this message of *'Hope'*, *'Restoration'*, *'Forgiveness' and 'Redemption'*.

My appreciation goes to my husband Colin Jackson for being a source of encouragement to me from the moment we met and even until now. I thank you for cooking all those great dinners for the family whilst I was working and praying to enable me to hear from God as we grew to embrace the reality of this book.

I am also thankful to all my children who are always ready to assist me when the need arises, for your love and support; it is a privilege for me to be your mother. You are the best!

My mother, I thank God for your life. To all my siblings thank you.

To *my* Pastor Dr Tayo Adeyemi who has raised me up, inspired me through his teaching and training. To Mrs. Joke Adeyemi you are an Angel. To the entire, Board of Ministers, Pastor Michael Olawore for your prayers, support and strength. Minister David Adabale, for all your support throughout this project. I could not have achieved this project without your support.

Betty Makoni for all your support, despite of
your busy schedule you made time for me.

I would also like to thank the following
wonderful people for their immense
contribution and support from the bottom of
my heart. The *'Against All Odds'* team, namely
Kemi Oyesola, Ekaete Inyang, Maria Runsewe,
Barry Trim, Remi Obasohan, Christopher
Obasohan, Sam Onigbanjo, Tola Onigbanjo,
Gabriel Olawande, Esther Olawande, Pamela
Obasa, Dr. Ify Ume, Betty Makoni. Yaw Off-
Boakez, Julie Odushile, Kate Oaihimire,
Lorraine Clarke and fiancé Clive McGhie and
Eric for producing the music for the CD,
Sabrina Carson USA, for designing both the
website, book covers front and back. To the
entire New Wine church leaders and members.
Thank you for all your support.

May God bless you all.

Foreword & Endorsement
by Betty Makoni

CNN Hero and UK Gender based violence Expert. Global Child Rights Hero, author, poet, mentor and Founder and Chief Executive Officer of Girl Child Network Worldwide. Betty Makoni has 32 global awards for excellence and innovation in advancing the rights of women and girls globally.

'Against All Odds..I Survived', by Fikelephi Jackson is a book I endorse after a thorough review. I have never read a story by an ordinary African woman who has never written before, yet Fikelephi takes the bold step of putting her story in print. I hereby present to the world the emergence of a 21st century African woman activist Fikelephi, who like many others, for years were invisible, ordinary and had become global statistics, massed as victims of domestic violence, of everyone and everything. This is to

announce that ordinary women like Fikelephi are coming out of their shells to tell their own stories, in their own style. They may not be as well-known as many of us but believe me, the women we built shelters for and regarded as powerless and voiceless have finally found their voice.

Fikelephi in her autobiography which is a simple, easy and yet intriguing and powerful story shows she is an ordinary woman who has transformed her life from that of a victim into a victor and now sets out on a journey to tell her story with the belief that it will change lives. She urges the world that it must learn from her life, a story told through her book. The self-made activist in her says she can put something on paper and then get friends to help her, so that women everywhere can be helped.

Fikelephi is a woman of strength, one the world should talk about. She is the invisible extraordinary woman whose story represents yet another forgotten generation of women who have waged and continue to wage war against domestic violence.

First, Fikelephi is a daughter of a political activist from a Political Party who decides to fight for his country. He is murdered before he could accomplish his mission, leaving behind his seven months pregnant wife. Little Fikelephi is symbolically left behind with her grandmother who becomes her guardian, one who is also in need of much support.

She grows up with a big question; *"where is my father and why did my mother leave me with a grandmother and took all her other children with her?"* That question was never answered for a long time. Later, she discovers her father died before he could free his country. This spurred her to bravely take up arms, go into war and continue the fight of her father. This is the generation of women political activists whose stories were never written.

Fikelephi brings us to the harsh realities of being in the war for justice as a woman and having to make the transition from war to normal life.

After the war, she is left to a rough rural life and provide for her education with the help of her grandmother. She becomes a girl who ends up mulled by an older man, who impregnates her and subjects her to the brutality of emotional and domestic violence. But through God's help, against all odds she arose from it all and emerged stronger and moved over to UK to join one of her sibling. She who was once labeled a failure, and disgrace, secured employment within UK after struggles with interviews.

Having left all her first three children in Africa she lived a life of a haunted immigrant. Her children were far away and so her love of a mother was strained. The father of her children, who was unmarried to her, did not want the children in her custody and so she had to fight for them to join her in the UK.

By then she had met a man who was a big promise for a safer and a more loving relationship, one who kept reassuring her to keep fighting for her children. After great loss of money, energy and time, her children got visas to join her in the UK. But tragedy struck when her daughter, a few months before she is due to start her degree at University, died tragically in a car accident. She was devastated and the consequences of the loss took its toll on her.

Against all odds is one book millions of women should read. It is short and written with simple language and imagery. It is an open testimony of a woman who willing to help thousands of women and girls who find themselves in similar situations. This book that will inspire them to share their story, changing lives. Fikelephi brings simple yet practical ways for women to begin the healing process from domestic violence and any past hurts. She has set up a place for many women come to as a place of safety and go through her trauma healing process. She listens to each one of them because no one does. The simple act of listening by someone with a deep understanding of what it means to be emotionally and physically abused is the most essential aspect of helping victims. This book will strategically mobilise women and girls in the UK and all over the world.

As I read through Fikelephi's story I realise that ordinary women are beginning to launch their own global campaign against domestic violence. In the case of Fikelephi she found love, a career, a home and children who are aspiring to greatness.

Fikelephi sends a powerful message to men and women stuck in domestic abuse and sex slavery to rise above the abuse and choose better lives. Yes she does admit that it is a difficult task, however giving up should not be an option because there is always a new day and beginning and with God all things are possible.

I personally recommend this book "Against All Odds." I believe it will be an empowerment tool for every woman who comes across it. Fikelephi holds your hand throughout her testimony. She asks you to see the other life ahead, shows you the odds she overcame and how and tells you not to get tired or give up but to keep going. I had thought by writing my own book I had done justice to issues affecting women but through Fikelephi's story I had to heal certain parts of me that were still aching. This is the last surgery I had to go through to relieve myself of my past trauma.

The book left me empowered, reassured and hopeful.   Throughout the story I became an activist cheering a woman fighting not just her own course but for those of others. In Fikelephi I see new leaderships on domestic violence emerging.

I fully endorse this book and recommend women to read and share with those they know will benefit from it.   I recommend all organisations working on domestic violence to embrace it as a story illustration when helping women come out of domestic violence.   I strongly recommend churches to add this book to church hymn book.

No one is born a victim; we are all victorious ~Betty Makoni

About Betty Makoni

Betty Makoni (BA Gen, BA Special Hons) is Founder and Chief Executive Officer of Girl Child Network Worldwide. Recently she was selected to be in the team of experts for Preventing Sexual Violence Initiative to be officially launched on 30 January 2013 by the UK Foreign Office. She joins the team as a Gender Based Violence expert. In her many high profile titles, millions across the world passionately call her CNN Hero as she was the top in 2009 category for Protecting the Powerless and was honoured by Goodwill Ambassador Nicole Kidman.

Betty Makoni might be the highest honoured and awarded African woman in the world with 32 local, regional and global awards for innovation, commitment and passion for her work to protect over 300,000 girls in Southern Africa. United Nations Red Ribbon award honoured Betty Makoni and Girl Child Network as having the most innovative strategy for gender equality. Betty Makoni is an Ashoka Fellow and singled out as one of the investors in poor and marginalised women and girls deserving of this life honour as a fellow. News Week named Betty as one of the 150 women who shake the world, alongside US Secretary of State Hillary Clinton. An Honorary Decade Child Rights Hero award (2011) that Betty Makoni received alongside President Nelson Mandela, who won the award, also shows the impact Betty Makoni has made globally.

Betty Makoni has inspired millions around the world to replicate the Girl Child Empowerment Model that she Developed. Besides her work with Girl Child Network Worldwide and building many Girl Child Networks in Africa and throughout the world, Betty Makoni is a mentor, coach, and trainer for women and girls who want to do similar work.

Betty has a lifetime of volunteerism and service to many causes and has served on Oxfam Novib and UNAIDS Round Tables. She sits on many boards of high profile organisations like RESTORED UK and serves as Ambassador and Patron of Africa

Achievers Award and Southern Africa Achievers Awards. Betty Makoni is the first woman to serve as Global Ambassador for UN 19 days of Activism for prevention of Child Abuse by Women World Summit an organisation with UN consultative status. Betty Makoni recently accepted to be Patron of UK based Malawi Women's Association, an organisation whose success she wants to see.

Betty Makoni is a published author of a poetry book, *A woman, Once a Girl: Breaking Silence,* which was recently launched in London. Her Autobiography Never Again, not on any woman or girl   http://bettymakoni.authorsxpress.com/ is inspiring women round the globe.

Betty Makoni is a hostess of a women and girls empowerment program on ZimPowerFM(www.zimpowerfm.com)every Sunday.

Betty is featured in best-selling books including *Women Who Light the Dark* by Paola Gianturco, *On The Up* by Nikki and Rob Wilson, as well as main subject in the award winning documentary, *Tapestries of Hope,* by U.S. Independent Presidential Hopeful for 2012, Michealene Risley. The Girl Child Network Empowerment Model which she started in 1998 has been singled out as Best Practice and included in University of Essex Journal for Human Rights 2010.

Website: (www.muzvarebettymakoni.org)

Endorsement by Michael Olawore

Senior Associate Minister, at New Wine Church, London, he is also the Executive Director New Wine International

Nicole Kidman says ... "One in three women may suffer from abuse and violence in her lifetime. This is an appalling human rights violation, yet it remains one of the invisible and under-recognized pandemics of our time." Violence against women is an appalling human rights violation. But it is not inevitable. We can put a stop to this."

Therefore if we must experience positive change in our society, we need people like **Fikelephi** to arise and give hope to the hopeless. And there could probably be no more opportune time than now, when we are being challenged to take responsibility for our communities and our society. The gauntlet has been laid down and the launch of **Against All Odds ...** is a timely and welcome response.

Fikelephi Jackson is one of our leaders at New Wine Church London. She serves as a Deputy Team Leader for the Cell Group Network within the church; she has been a tremendous asset to New Wine Church and consequently to the community that we serve.

Fikelephi is highly inspirational and motivational in her leadership approach. She has been a positive influence in the lives of the people that she leads. Fikelephi has a heart for God's people and a passion to serve others in fulfilling their God ordained purpose. It is this passion that has birthed **Against all Odds ...**

For too long, we have discussed the problem; I am thrilled that we are finally rolling up our sleeves and preparing to produce sustainable solutions. Someone once said it is better to light a candle than to curse the darkness.

Thank you, Fikelephi, for lighting a candle. May the light and flame of this little candle be fanned into a mighty conflagration, and may this candle light many more, until darkness is completely obliterated from our land.

Endorsement by Minister David Adebale
New Wine Church – London UK

'Against All Odds' book is an incredible tool that will transform and inspire you regardless of the challenges you are facing right now. An amazing story of what God can do when all hope is lost, all options exhausted, discouraged to the lowest point and the future looks bleak.

About Fikelephi Jackson: I have known Fikelephi for almost 10 years and found her to be a woman of integrity, incredible faith, trustworthy and with a very large heart, she always strives to add value to everyone she comes in contact with. You will never imagine that such a person who has experience a past of pain, hurt and abuse can live a happy life as a wife, mother and mentor with pastoral care over hundreds of people. Her story is truly remarkable and you too will be inspired to overcome the challenges of life.

The book Against All Odds carries a message of *hope, restoration and forgiveness.* *The* story of this incredible lady will inspire and motivate you to press forward with your life **'against all odds'.**

Profile: Minister David is an executive coach as well as Director of Outreach and Media operations at the London-based charity New Wine where he oversees a team of 90 that produces an average of 460 TV and 680 Radio programs every year to a worldwide audience. Using his over 15 years in leadership, he coach's executives in successful careers without losing everything and everyone. His overriding passion to help individuals maximise their lives through the effective and efficient utilisation of their talents, time and treasures. In 2011 he launched Systems4Living.com featuring a number of online educational training programs and materials. His seminars and coaching programs have been called "life transforming" enjoyed by graduates, entrepreneurs and executives.

Table of Contents

PROLOGUE

She is a daughter of a political activist from a Political Party who decides to fight for his country. He, her father is murdered before he could accomplish his mission, leaving behind his seven months pregnant wife. Little Fike is symbolically left behind with her grandmother who becomes her guardian; one who is also in need of much support. She grows up with the burning question; *"who and where is my father and why did my parents leave me with a grandmother and took all their other children with them?"* That question was never answered for a long time, however, she later discovers her father died before he could free his country and before she was born. This spurred her on to take up arms, go into war and continue the fight from where her father left off.

After the war, she is left to a rough rural life and the continuation of her education. She becomes a girl who ends up mulled by an older man, who impregnates her and subjects her to the brutality of emotional and domestic violence. But through God's help, against all odds she arose from it all and emerged stronger and better. She who was once labeled a failure, and disgrace, secured employment within UK with new opportunities to change her life around. But having left all her first three children in Africa, she lived a life of a haunted immigrant. Her children were far away and so her love of a mother was strained. The father of her children, who was unmarried to her, did not want the children in her custody and so she had to fight for them to join her in the UK. By then she had met a man who was a big promise for a safer and a more loving relationship, one who kept reassuring her to keep fighting for her children.

This is her story of how she overcame the stigma and trauma of domestic violence, to become the voice of many women, to encourage them that against all odds, they too with God's help can be free from a life of emotional and physical abuse

By Betty Makoni

Fike & Her Mum

CHAPTER 1

It's A Girl!

Let me tell you what my mother told me about the events surrounding my birth.

"It was one fine morning. It was on the 23rd April 1963,"she paused, struggling to bring the words out. I could feel her breaking down.

"I had nothing, not even a nappy and could not think of what I would put on you after birth. I knew I was going to hospital to meet other women pampered by their husbands with just everything. I was actually 9 months pregnant – at full term. I had no choice. Selling beer was the only way I could get some income. Only a little to make sure you come into the world and have something. The money being raised was to pay for the hospital bills and to also buy a few baby things; you know nappies, clothes and so on," my mother started to tear inside her heart and then her eyes became watery. I knew the pain of being the only one of the two parents when a child comes was too much to bear for her.

Now, I know what you must be asking yourself reader, 'Where on earth, where was her father who under normal situation could have been expected to be by her mother's side emotionally, economically and physically?'

My father died three months before I was born, leaving my Mother with six other children.

"Coming back to this special day on 23rd of April, I worked the whole day until I felt something strange, it was a pain about, well, below my abdomen. My waters broke whilst I gave my customer some beer. I had no slight idea you were coming. Any woman will tell you, Fikelephi, that when it comes to labour pains, it's unstoppable; You can't say, 'I am not ready today'. When the time comes, that is it. But I wanted to raise more money so that my baby has something," said my mother.

Each time I think about this, I wonder how much a woman could take. I also wonder how my mother had developed coping mechanisms that made her so resilient.   You see, she had just lost her husband and in our culture back in South Africa, she would have been in mourning and people would have noticed because she was required to wear a black scarf.

At the same time she went through the pain of losing my father, she was in labour pains to bring me in the world and labouring every hour in whilst still doing business selling beer right up until now, the waters signalled my coming, she was expecting me, her seventh child.   A child normally brings joy to the family. So how was my Mother dealing with both emotions – sadness and joy? Also, she told me that my Father was the sole bread winner of the family.

No wonder she had to sell beer. She had six children already and the seventh one was on its way. What a difficult time she found herself in. Those were indeed hard times. As I reflect today, I really wonder how she lived through it all.

"I realised I was in labour because my waters broke. My sister-in-law took me to the nearest hut because I couldn't walk. A few other ladies helped. In the hut, my mother was waiting as she had gone ahead to put together a make shift maternity ward. She had cut up old blankets into four pieces to make nappies. She had also prepared hot water and other things to help deliver the baby. Because I had been busy all day, labour was not very long. Shortly after getting into the hut, my mother delivered the baby. "It's a girl!" shouted my mother.

"Fikelephi, that's how you were born."

My grandmother gave me the name, Fikelephi which means 'you have brought us joy despite losing your father.' Or you have brought many blessings.'

There were seven of us to be fed. My mother never took some time to rest or to heal as expected. She made plans to leave me with grandma as she went to the city. Only my two brothers and four sisters who were older left the village with her. I was given to my grandmother and she assumed the role of my mother.

At the time, as I grew up, I felt a sense of rejection. I felt that my mother had abandoned me. Or is it poverty that made my mother break the physical and emotional bond? I know poverty leaves one at the deep end of life. For me and my mother we just broke our relationship when I was a baby. There is a child in me that make me think my mother did not like me at all. Nothing could have justified taking all my older siblings and leaving me with grandmother. I felt like she did not want me. Why didn't she take me as well? Why did God take my Father away too? I had so many questions which got no answers. But like any child, I wanted to know.

War Broke Out!

My mother was emotionally so close to me because she made it a routine to come at least three times a year. She came to the village with goodies like food, clothes and anything that would cheer a little girl. I started to understand who she was. An absent mother who cared but whose trolley of life was filled with responsibilities for seven children. She had to divide herself between six children in the city and one in the village. She honoured her promise to supply basics.

In reality I had two mothers; my biological mother who supplied goodies and my grandmother who was emotionally attached to me. My grandmother never left the village. She was born in Swaziland. She raised her own children including my mother in Southern Africa. Now she was raising her children's child. Such resilience to repeat mother's role was amazing.

So there I was with my grandmother. She was a true extension of my mother in every sense. She provided for my emotional needs. I called her mother emotionally and grandmother physically. My grandmother lived in the village and brought me up in the village. For some reason, I think; when everything earthly had gone, she found faith in God. She found her soul at peace and well supplied when she called her God. If there is anything that I learnt as a child was to know God was the father. My grandmother had found solace and religion had given her everything. She gave me so much love and taught me what she knew about God because she was a devoted Christian and a deaconess in the Methodist church she attended. I couldn't have been brought up any better – although I still missed my mother.

The start of going to Jabatshaba Primary School brings painful memories. I was a poverty stricken child who had to brace during winter with feet frozen in the cold. I had no jersey and nothing to warm myself with clothing. I did not like going to school because this meant removing myself from the fire in grandma`s hut which I had been used to. I still recall how thorny the road were and each time I walked to and from school I had to figure out how to keep my little shoeless feet from being harmed. The distance to school was too long. It was a daily struggle. I tried to think of the best way to make the distance shorter.

As if that was not enough I found myself working on a farm where I had to take charge of livestock. Reader, now picture myself having to chase after goats, cows and sheep and any slightest mistake to lose one or cause injury to any of them would land me in big trouble. Besides this hard labour in the valleys where cattle did grazing, I had to give to some help to work on the fields where we planted seeds. It was a dawn to dusk job. It required you not to watch the clock but to watch when the job is done. We always ended the day with everyone limping as our feet were been overstrained. The farmers overused us to an extent that I accepted to be but one of the unfortunate children who remained invisible in the continent.

The war ravaged many villages. It was the news we heard about. There were many stories of those who had disappeared. News came about those who had run away from the villages. The news was about death. There was bloodshed. The country had taken to war and news came about those who sacrificed themselves and gave their lives. I was a teenage girl by then. I had my emotional war going on of losing a mother to the city and then a father to death. Those two wars would never end. Besides, I had puberty to face as another war. For sure how many emotional and physically wars was I in? The wars were becoming countless for me. It was the 1970s in then Rhodesia when war had broken out. Families, villages, people and just everything just broke down and came to a standstill. There was so much anger and hate. People were dying everywhere.

Menstruation had commenced and it was never understood by me even at age 16. Moreover, it was a taboo subject.

"His name was Dave and was a very distinguished gentleman and was very, very handsome. He always wore suits and was a very hard working man which is why your mother did not have to work while he was alive. Your hair is a bit like your   paternal grandmother's," said my grandmother.

Like Nelson Mandela and Steve Biko, my father was detained as a political prisoner. Black people suffered in South Africa and ANC was the political party he belonged to. Apartheid killed my father. Apartheid has a victim in me as a child. My father suffered bleeding when he came out of prison. After three months he died.

The news about my father's death devastated me. He died fighting. He died whilst on way to liberate the masses. Who was going to replace my father as a liberator? My father was calling her daughter to duty. Whatever he did not fulfil as a liberator, I was going to do it myself. They say like mother like daughter but today as I thought of taking up the struggle my father left I just told myself like father like daughter. I wanted to fulfil my father`s legacy. I wanted to fight from where he had left this struggle. I was ready. I was not going to be a spectator at all. I told myself to win a battle one must fight. The fact that my father died fighting told me he must have taken liberating people to be very important. My father`s footprints would not be rubbed from history. Yes, I knew I was female. By then society made females not to look up to their fathers. But how could a liberator die and her daughter not continue his legacy?

At age 15 I found myself Chair of the political party. I felt I was growing up to be a political activist. At this age we were not allowed to carry guns as there was age limit. There were many guerrilla tactics was actively involved; instead we used our voices as weapons and followed through with action. We did not move around as a group but in pairs so that we were not easily noticeable. It was during one of these patrols that two members of my party came upon a freedom fighter, who had been shot. They bound up his wounds as best as teenagers could and came to find me and the others. So we developed a strategy where we took turns going to take care of him so that we did not bring attention to ourselves or to him.

His survival was in our hands even though we were not doctors and did not even have any First Aid experience, we had to look after this brave soldier. We had to nurse his wounds, feed him and above all hide him.

Shortly after meeting and taking care of the freedom fighter, we decided to visit 2 youths who were brother and sister. We had rumours that they had exposed us to the opposing party. I led my group to their house on condition that all we would do was to speak with them, not hurt them in any way. I had an agreement with the boys in my group. When we got there we spoke with them and tried to elicit information from them but they were not forthcoming. Suddenly, the boys who had agreed with me not to hurt them began whipping them, they eventually confessed that they had become traitors and our lives were in danger.

The opposing party knew we were around and were also hiding something. They did not have accurate information that we were nursing a freedom fighter. We had become the hunted and went into hiding just like the freedom fighter.

This meant that the opposing party also knew that there were freedom fighters around our village area. We were the target; and as far as everyone was concerned we knew everything. Once again innocent people were being tortured, even killed, and houses were being burnt down.

After having a serious meeting with the freedom fighter it became apparent that we had to leave the country as soon as possible, or else we were going to be killed, tortured or locked up in jail. That was the last thing I needed, I did not want to go through what my father went through at all. I had no other choice; I had to leave the country.

Road to Freedom

My few belongings took me a short time to bundle. I had not much to pack. I was more worried about emotionally packing I was supposed to do. Someone had to know where I was going and so the only person I confided in was my grandmother. She prayed for me and the prayer became my spiritual guidance. I felt strengthened. I thanked my grandmother for praying for me. She prayed for me and said she believed that I would be guided on my road to freedom.

Going to join the liberation war was the only option I had under the circumstances. My father had left the job incomplete and so it was time I took it up. I knew my life would never be the same. My life was about to change dramatically. I was not so sure what was about to happen to me. In today's society, at 15, a young person would say this situation was 'freaking them out'; and I was really freaking out.

David, the freedom fighter was there to guide us on the road to freedom. He is the one who taught us to travel using the rising and setting of the sun. He told us all the girls had to wear trousers otherwise as we travel, the thorns in the bushes would bruise us. And in those days, in our culture in the village, girls did not wear trousers. But in this case, culture was thrown out of the window; we girls had to wear trousers for our survival. All the boys had to give a pair of trousers to the girls.

After this meeting with David, uncertain about the journey that lay ahead of us and what we were to face – this was a life or death situation as we had heard that most youth trying to cross the borders were either killed or detained. So we decided to take a chance. Although we were over a 100, some chose not to leave the country with reasons like, 'I want to have an education'; 'I am afraid I will not make it'; 'I don't want to leave my family' and other such excuses. So, just 80 of us along with David, the freedom fighter started out on this journey. We did not take any food or drink with us. There was no time to plan this; the decision to leave took place in the morning; we were by no means organised enough to take any form of subsistence with us.

We left our village late in the afternoon. We all had to walk in a straight line with the freedom fighter in front of us. In the meeting that followed David and I were appointed commanders of the group. I became the Deputy Commander. We walked for two days without food water or anything at all. We kept hoping that soon we were going to come across a village or some water at least because we were thirsty, hungry and terrified of what dangers lay ahead of us.

On our third day, late in the afternoon, we came across a fruit tree known as Umpumpulwane – it is a little golden yellow fruit when it is ripe and green when unripe, the size of a blackberry and tastes sweet like a cross between a tangerine and an orange. David told us it was safe to eat it, but the only catch was that after eating it, we would be thirsty. What choice did we have? We all saw this fruit as a lifesaver as we were desperately hungry. We hadn't had anything in 3 days. So we ate the fruit.

At this time we learnt that we still had about 15 miles to go before the next village, this was not good news as I could barely walk, my feet were throbbing with soreness, it was very hot and most of all I was thirsty. The 15 miles was really just an estimate as David explained to us that we had to go over this and that mountain. It definitely would have been much more than 15 miles.

One of the girls became very ill she couldn't open her eyes much less walk. We all had to take a break until she was well enough to walk at least to next village. Others fell ill and were weak and faint, but not as badly as this girl was. I kept praying and pleading for God not to let us die in the wilderness. And this time, I actually prayed.   Thank God for my grandmother who taught me how to pray even though I had little or no faith. I just did it with the hope that it will work.

Finally, we saw smoke afar. Hooray! It was the next village. I had a few thoughts: What if the villagers would not have us? What if they call the soldiers to come and kill us? Oh! The questions were endless; there was this feeling of great insecurity. I know sometimes when we are going through challenges, all we can do is take one day at a time; but in this situation, I could only take ONE HOUR at a time.

It was very clear that anything could happen to us and nobody will ever know what happened to us. We did not tell anyone where we were going because we did not know where we were going. All we knew was we had to survive, we had to save our lives. I, for one, was not going to die at the hands of the opposing party like my father did. Even then, I was very terrified.

Thank God our freedom fighter had connections in this area. As soon as we arrived, once they recognised it was David, they were very warm and hospitable towards us all. In no time, the leader of the village organised that the villagers cook a lot of food for us, so within few hours, which felt like 12 hours to me as I and my group were so, so hungry, we had food coming from different homes. We ate heartily and very quickly.   We ate like there was no tomorrow. You can imagine how the boys among us ate; if the girls were not quick, we would have remained hungry even after eating, as there may not have been enough food.   It was the most glorious time of my short life – food after 3 days, real food!

After the meal, some of the elders came with traditional African herbal remedies and the women among them came with warm water. With these, they cleaned our wounds; this was very welcome especially those of us like me who had very sore feet.   They admired us for our bravery especially considering how young we all were and encouraged us to continue to fight for our country. Some of these elders were parents who had already lost their teenage sons and daughters to death during the war.

I am sure that you are wondering what young people had to do with the war. Why were they being killed? They were not soldiers. Well the only answer I had then was that we were vulnerable and could easily be caught and tortured for information. So we were constantly a target. We spent one night resting and feasting like we have never eaten before.

I lay awake that night thinking to myself 'what are you letting yourself into?'

What amazed me was this; seeing the desperate expressions on the faces of the elders and other villagers and having their support. Having their support was very encouraging. It was written all over their faces that we the young generation were the future and were the hope for the nation.

That made me even more determined to go out there and fight for freedom; I knew in my heart that I had made a tough but right decision; not that I had any choice.

The following morning we left the village to carry on in our journey which was going to take us 10 days in the wilderness. Yes, it was the wilderness. All we had for company were wild animals and birds, but mostly birds.

What followed was a lot of near death experiences; helicopters hovering over our heads looking for a freedom fighter with a lot of youths. By this time our number had increased from 80 to about 120 youths. We had been joined by other youths from the village where we had spent the night. The opposing party knew that we were so many and thought it would be easier to locate us as it would be harder to hide such a huge number of people. This just tells you that the whole nation knew that situation was not getting any better; it was war.

At the end of the 10-day journey, we found ourselves over the border in a nearby country. They had opened their borders for such battalion like us and had freedom fighters in hiding who would help us once we crossed over. David knew exactly where they would be hiding and led us to them. They took us to individual girls and boys camps. And this is where I spent the next couple of years as a teenage girl.

I lived in a girl's camp, living like a prisoner, waking up at 5am each day and going on lots of parades and training exercises. This was where we were trained to be soldiers. We used to do an exercise known as 'toyitoyi' (pronounced 'doyeedoyee'). This was a bitter-sweet march with the leader inspiring us to fight for our rights and for what is right by chanting words like: 'are you going let them beat you?' 'Fight for your rights, fight for what is right!' 'We can do this!' And we would answer with the word, 'toyitoyi' meaning, yes, we shall fight, we shall not give up. It was like a dance and a march all at the same time. This was fun because it helped me to ventilate and exercise all at the same time.

The part that was not fun was if one of us did something wrong. We would be punished by being told to do high numbers of press ups or other exercises that would hurt. And we did this in the hot, burning sun.

But what was even worse was that people fell ill. And the diseases were usually contagious, like cholera and others like it. As you can imagine, good hygiene was not a priority. Things like water to wash were very scarce. We had water, the amount that would fill a medium sized baked bean tin to wash my body; so I would wash the important parts of my body. We ate once a day. We would queue up to go and collect our meals when our brigades were called out. In each battalion were a commander and a deputy.

After the exercise, all the battalion will come together for a parade after which the camp commander would brief us on the current happenings of the war. The worst thing I thought, was watching my fellow comrades die every day.

Also, that there was no way of knowing if my family was still alive and neither was there a way of them knowing if I was still alive as people were dying in hundreds and thousands and camps were bombed by the opposing party very frequently. My days in the camp ended

Against All Odds I Survived

without my ever having to go out to fight and physically kill people. For this, I was thankful.

At Last It's Over ... But Is It?

Thank God, in the 1980's there was a 'cease fire' and we were finally released to go back home. This was a very daunting time for all of us. We had mixed feelings we did not even know if our parents and friends had survived the war or not. No matter how brave anyone is there comes a time when reality hits you. Some of my fellow comrades got to find out that every member of their family had been killed during the war. Those who didn't die had become disabled, with broken legs and arms, paralysed in wheel chairs because they had been tortured in jail; I could go on.... Oh there was so much pain, hurt and sadness for many. Yet on the other hand, some found their families had survived and they were alive and well.

I was yet to find out what had become of my family, I must admit I was a bit scared even to find out. After the army trucks had dropped me off in my village, I looked for and found my grandmother who was still alive. She was so overwhelmed when she saw me, that she wept with joy.

Then there was the big question? I could not wait to ask grandmother about my mother; was she still alive? What about my brothers and sisters? Thank goodness I did not have to wait any longer before I got answers to my questions.

Yes, my mother was still alive. She remained in the city although her home was burnt down – the one that she built in the village. The opposing party came looking for my mother not my grandmother. Not finding her, they burnt and destroyed her home. If they had found her, they would have killed her, as a direct result of them knowing from the traitors' that some children had left to fight in the war.

Some of my friend's parents were killed by first tying them up in the house and setting the house on fire. As my grandmother told me these stories, my blood would go cold; I could not stop crying, oh, it hurt so much.

I stayed with my grandmother for about 2 weeks before leaving to see my mother. This was because there was no way of communicating to my mother that I was safe and sound and had returned home. So she felt the earlier I travelled to see my mother and siblings the better as she was sure that my mother was very anxious to see me. It was all over the news that we had returned. After all, the war was over...but was it?

Finally, I was able to go to the city where my mother and the rest of my brothers and sisters were. It was in the afternoon when I arrived, it was almost as if I was dreaming, now that I knew my mother was alive as were my brothers and sisters. I went to my mother's house but she was not home as she was out running her business. She had a stall selling food and vegetables.

When I arrived, at first she couldn't recognise me. Suddenly she realised who I was. Her long 'lost' daughter whom she thought was dead and would never see again.

Once again, I cried tears of joy as we hugged. I was filled with emotion and overwhelmed with gladness at the reality of being with my mum once again... after such a long time. It had been three years of pain, fear, terror, loneliness, confusion and so many other emotions; many of which I did not understand and could not handle. After crying and screaming and talking, all at the same time, I went off to meet my brothers and sisters. That in itself was a happy reunion although I did not really know them.   But I was glad to be with my family again.

I do not quite remember how long I was in the city before I began to think about my future. Maybe it was six months or so. Soon I started questioning myself. Fair enough the war was over but it wasn't really over. It was time to fight for who we had become as a people and who we wanted to become – the battle had only just began.

While some of my friends felt this was the time to party, I began thinking about more serious things like my education. I did not have any qualifications apart from the basic primary education. I knew I had to do something very fast. Although I was now with my mother whom I expected to provide for me, I knew that she could not afford the High School fees, for in Southern Africa; secondary school education was paid for. So how on earth was I going to obtain my education? I was 17 years old then. I began talking to my friends about going to back for further education, they thought I was mad. They saw this time as an opportunity for them to live the teenage life that we had all obviously missed.

One thing I learnt during those hard times was this **'time is so precious'.** One of the contagious diseases that ravaged the girls camp was someone would wake up complaining of having a headache. The person would throw up a few times and usually by afternoon of the same day, the person would be dead. I never knew what that disease was called but I knew that I never caught the disease. Time is really so precious.

I knew that I had to move forward and stop moaning about my missed childhood and teenage years. I knew I had to do first things first; I had to get my education sorted out.

CHAPTER 2

Would anyone please give me a chance?

Despite what my friends thought of me, I knew I was on the right track. Something or someone had decided to give me a chance to live and it must have been for a reason. So I began to speak to officials and discovered that there were scholarships being awarded to young people who had gone to war and who had a desire to return to school. I had to go through all the formalities before being sent to boarding school – Mtshabezi Secondary School, near Gwanda.

I was excited about the prospect of returning to school. Most of my friends wondered what the big deal was; after all it was only school and there were many other exciting things to do. Over the next four years, I integrated into the school.

The first year was very daunting. First, we were a little older than most of the other students and I was in a proper classroom with desks.

My last classroom was under a tree as a primary school student in the village. So this was very different. I had so much to adjust to; the discipline, being in boarding school and although a mixed school, the girls had separate dormitories to the boys. The diet was different too but most of the other students were used to it. We ate meat or chicken once a week and ate vegetables often. The same meal was repeated for four days but it was still a treat to me as I had never eaten this well before.

I made new friends in the first year. Study-wise, I was doing well with most subjects but struggled with mathematics. But in my eyes, it was good struggle.

In the third year, I started two subjects, Cookery and Fashion & Fabrics. These were my favourite subjects as it brought out the creativity in me which I enjoyed very much and I won many awards in these subjects.

It was a well sought after Christian school so there were many children from wealthy families who attended the school as well. I felt I was different because I didn't have that kind of well-to-do upbringing. Most of the girls had boyfriends and their parents gave them a lot of money compared to what I had. Because I was so focused on my studies, boys were the last thing on my mind. I knew that one day I would get married, but education came first for me for now.

These four years involved a lot of hard work; I knew I had to do well in my 'O' Levels, after which I wanted to go to America. I dreamt of being able to buy my mother a big house. I enjoyed school a lot but it was nice to go home over the school holidays.

Girls Just Want To Have Fun!

Isn't it amazing when you think of the amount of pressure young people are under, these days:

pressure to excel in their studies; pressure to be part of a certain circle of friends; pressure to be accepted by society; pressure to date; and the list goes on. I was not immune to all these pressures, most of my friends had boyfriends and they made it seem as though girls like me were abnormal. Eventually, I thought maybe they were right and I should at least date someone; go to the movies, or out to dinner. Looking back, that was such a naïve thought.

In my last year when I was to take my 'O' Level exams, I made up my mind that I was going to find a boy – nothing serious, just someone to go out and have fun with for a change. I did meet someone. His name was Suli and he was ten years older than me.

I met him during the school holidays. There were quite a few guys who had been watching me and Suli was one of them. But I didn't know this then. One day, I was on my way to the library; he stopped in his car and asked me where I was going and gave me a lift. During the ride, he told me how he had been watching me and how much he liked me.   Before he dropped me off at the library, he asked me if I would like to go and watch a film with him.   Of course, I said yes. We planned to go out during the next school holiday as I was about to travel back to school for the next term.

When Suli asked me out, I thought that with a date sorted I would have something to talk about when I got back to school.   Little did I know that this was to be a turning point in my life. We should be careful what we wish for.

During the next set of school holidays, when we were to go out to the cinema, I had let Suli know that I was not the kind of girl to sleep around with boys. He assured me that I would be safe and to put my heart at rest, on the day we would be going to the cinema, his uncle would come along with him in the car to pick me up.

On the day we went out to the cinema, or at least we planned to. For some reason we were delayed and by the time we got to the cinema we had missed the film. My new-found boyfriend suggested we go to dinner and come back for the midnight show. That sounded good and I agreed. While I was excited about going to dinner, I was a bit concerned about how late the film would finish. However, Suli's uncle assured me they were going to take me home afterwards.

Too Late To Regret!

I must say that for some reason on this particular date I felt a bit nervous. It was as if I could hear two voices; one saying, 'go on the date, his uncle will protect you if he tries to do anything you don't want' and the other quieter voice saying, 'don't go, there is danger ahead, this is no ordinary day.' But I went all the same.

After the film, my date and his uncle took me to the car, but as we drove off I noticed that we were headed in the wrong direction. I asked what was happening and it turned out we were passing through Suli's flat as his uncle wanted to pick something up before he dropped me home. When we got to his flat, Suli's uncle insisted I come in for a few minutes. I agreed because it was the early hours of the morning and I could understand that he did not want me waiting in the car on my own at that time of the night.

While inside I waited in the living room, and before I knew it I heard the sound of the car driving off. I remember thinking to myself that it could not be the uncle. How wrong was I, it was his uncle, he had actually left me behind. Suli walks back into the living room from the part of the house he had been. I asked him which car just drove off. And he said it was his uncle.

I was really angry. I asked why his uncle had left me. Was he coming back to pick me up? Suli wondered why I was angry after all, he said I was under a roof, not outside and I was safe. I reminded him that was not the plan we agreed on, his uncle was to take me home. Obviously I had to spend the night at Suli's flat; the rest, as they say, is history.

Suli left me again in the living room and I dozed off on the chair. But I had began to smell something like cigarette smoked, I did not know Suli that he smoked. I was not alarmed, however, I did not like it, as this triggered headaches.

Later, I do not know how much later, Suli came back to the living room and said I could not sleep on the sofa; I should go to his bed and lie down. And he would sleep on the sofa. And that was fine by me as by this time I was really tired and wanted to go to sleep. Albeit, that niggling voice saying something is wrong. But I went to sleep on the bed anyway. I was just so tired.

Shortly after I lay down, he came to lie down beside me. I told him he couldn't but he said there was no point his sleeping on the sofa when there was a bed available and anyway, he said, 'I have told you that I like you, so what is the problem?' One thing led to another and Suli ended up having sex with me that night against my wishes.

Three months later when the school holidays were over, I went back to school with a story to tell but I couldn't help being in two minds about my date. Although I was excited about the date, it had been overshadowed by what happened that night in his flat. I felt so bad and somehow I knew that my life would never be the same again. It was too late to regret, I told myself, I still had a chance to change things and so I focused on my studies again. I decided I was going to end this 'thing' with Suli

I could not even call it a relationship as it was non-existent in the first place.

Remember, I hardly knew him. And as I previously stated, I was not interested in having a boyfriend neither did he appeal to me in that way.

After lessons one day, I called him and asked if I could speak to him in person, to which he eagerly agreed. When I met him I told him that I made a mistake in going out with him. I just wanted to have a bit of fun, and was not ready to start any kind of relationship as I really wanted to pursue my education. I apologised. He looked at me and smiled. "Are you sure you want to end this?" he asked. Of course I was sure. I did not understand why at the time, he kept glancing at my tummy and asking if I was okay. When he left he told me he has a feeling that I might need him sooner than I realised.

It did not make sense to me why on earth he would think that I would need him and that worried me slightly. Nevertheless I left that day with a sense of achievement, feeling so relieved that our 'relationship' was over. I hoped and prayed that I would never need him in anyway. It was during the school holidays that I became very ill and my sister had to take me to the doctors who ran a few tests. The results came back. The diagnosis: I was pregnant.

I did not know what to do with myself. I was terrified! How was I going to break this to my mum? My sister who took me to the doctors knew my desire to be educated and become a citizen of good character, so she had a sense of how I was feeling. I felt it would be better for the earth to open up and swallow me than to live with the thought of breaking the news to my mother whom I had already put through so much. Plus, the fact that I was the first of her children who had made it to secondary school, all my older siblings attended primary school only. I cried and cried buckets of tears. What was I going to do?

At that moment it became very apparent that Suli knew what he was talking about, when he said that I would need him someday soon.

I called him to break the news and he was over the moon. He left what he was doing and came straight over to us outside the doctor's clinic. He came out of his car and came to meet us. I was beside myself and still could not really talk. I was more concerned about the fact that I did not know this man. So, he told us to come to his car and that he would take us home. But then my sister began to tell him how she noticed I was not eating as I usually would when I came home for the holidays and how I became very sick and now it has been diagnosed that I am pregnant. Suli said I should not be upset because he would be with me and he would take responsibility. He started planning how he would need to speak to his family and meet with mine.

I was disappointed with myself.

Baby Dave

CHAPTER 3

Becoming a Mum

Things changed very fast for me and I was very confused. One of my main concerns was that I did not know Suli very well. I had only just met him, broken up with him and now he was to be the father of my child. Oh my goodness, the baby! There was another person involved in all my feeling bad and it had nothing to do with how bad I was feeling really; it had to do with the new life that was growing on the inside of me. How much worse can any situation become? The silver lining though, was that I had just finished writing my 'O' Level examinations.

In Zulu/Indebele tribe, the culture is that a girl's jaha (the potential son-in-law) has to approach the family through a mediator (idombo) to propose. If both families approve, especially the girl's family, then they would say how many cows, or how much money has to be paid for the Lobola (dowry).

Sadly, things were a little different in my case.

Eventually, both families got to meet, with my brother representing my dad. Another interesting thing about my culture is that they have a lot of respect for babies, even unborn ones. Because of this, nothing was to be discussed as far as the Lobola was concerned; the only thing my family wanted to know was Suli's intentions – to marry me, or sponsor the baby? He answered that his intention was to marry me once the baby was born.

This was a nightmare for me. It's one thing meeting someone and getting to know them. But it's a different story when you've just met a person, you just ended a relationship that had technically not even started, and then all of a sudden you find that you're having their child. Why did life have to be so difficult for me, why did it have to be so abnormal? Why wasn't I born in a normal hospital, with mum and dad and everything else that goes with it. Grow up normally, go to a proper school then college then graduate and then get married. I had to fight for every little thing from birth, could somebody tell me why? Why? Why? I had so many 'Whys'.

Either way the damage had already been done and I had to lay aside my feelings, intentions and even my dreams as I now had a baby on the way to think about.

I refer to this as 'damage' because that is the way people in my tribe refer to situations like mine.

Again in my culture, in these cases where the pregnancy was unplanned, a certain amount of money or number of cows was charged to the father-to-be; this was announced and Suli and his mediator were told that the rest would be discussed after the birth of the baby. Even though this is what should happen, Suli didn't pay anything.

Now you can imagine my frustrations. But things had to be different; I now had someone who I was responsible for - my baby in my own womb, a precious baby who was not to be blamed for my mistakes. Part of me began to be excited about having a baby; what were he/she going to look like what would they grow up to become?

I had begun to feel some movement in my abdomen; I would have cravings for all sorts of foods.

It was then that I made up my mind to do everything in my power to make sure that my baby was okay. I was going to be the best mum for him or her. I knew that this was not going to be easy but I had made my bed and so I had to lie on it.

I started knitting bits and pieces just like any pregnant mum would do. I used to talk a lot to my unborn baby, promising him/her that I was looking forward to seeing them, holding them. Even though I was very uncertain about what the future held in store for my baby's father and I, I planned to be there for my baby no matter what the outcome was.

Time flew by and before I knew it I had reached full-term and I got increasingly nervous with all the stories I had heard about the pain of childbirth. My wish however was that I would have my baby in a proper hospital, not in a hut like my mum. I had registered with one of the best hospitals in the city, at least that was something.

During the late stages of my pregnancy I was staying at my sister's house even though Suli had asked me to move in with him – I was not particularly keen on moving in with him just yet.

My mum was in England with my eldest sister, Linda, looking after her children when I fell pregnant. A letter was written by my sister, Stella, who I was living with to my mum. Linda replied on the behalf of my mum. She was not happy at all. She wanted more information about how it all happened and about who Suli was and his family.

I will never know how my mum really felt about it. In those days we did not have access to phones or things like that and my mum did not write letters.

I just felt that I had disappointed her so many times over the years and this was just another disappointment. What can I say?

One day I had an appointment at the doctor's clinic but had to pass by Suli's flat to collect some papers. I was very shocked to find a girl sitting on his bed. I introduced myself to her and she introduced herself to me. I told her I was expecting Suli's child and she told me that she was Suli's girlfriend.

I was now even more upset that I allowed myself to get into this situation. Unfortunately my back was now against the wall; I felt trapped. I realised then that my instincts back on our first date were right; there was something not quite right about Suli. When Suli got home, his 'girlfriend' told him of my visit. He apologised to me, and promised to end the relationship with her.

Giving Birth

Finally I gave birth to a beautiful baby boy. He was so cute and I could not believe that despite my situation this child could bring me so much joy, so much hope and love.

The months that followed were very busy, the sleepless nights, and so on. But they were worth it because he was so gorgeous. He was the only beautiful thing I had in my whole life which is why I do not regret having him.

I had a scheduled post-natal appointment in the hospital one day when Dave was about six or seven months old. When I got there, the staff nurse noticed that Dave was very healthy and I was very lucky and happy to have him. But she also noticed that I did not have a wedding ring on. So after the appointment, she began speaking to me. She was the first older person to really give advice about life aside from my grandmother.

She asked me if I was married, I said no. She asked if I was living with the father of my child. I told her that I was. She asked if I wanted to be pregnant again. I told her I did not want to because I wanted to go back and finish my education, do my A levels and go further.

She was glad that I was telling the truth but also noticed that I was not happy living with Suli.   So she gave me some tablets and explained to me that they were contraceptive tablets.   She explained that I was to take them every day at the same time and not to miss a single day otherwise I would fall pregnant.

So, I went home.   When I got home, Suli asked me how the appointment went.

I told him it went well and being naïve, I also told him about my conversation with the staff nurse and showed him the contraceptive tablets, 30 of them that she gave me to use.   I did not expect what happened next.   I had put Dave down; he could sit by himself and was crawling.

As I reached for my bag to show Suli the tablets and the baby book, Suli got very angry as I carried on telling him how things went in the hospital. He rolled up his sleeves and the expression on his face was one of intense anger and rage. "How dare you do that? Who told you to get those tablets? I decide when you have babies or not!"

I had never seen Suli like this before. This was another side to him I was totally unaware of. He took me into a room, picked up the extension cord used to plug in electrical devices and began to beat me with it. I was screaming and crying, begging him to stop. Dave heard me and started to cry.

Suli simply took me into another room, far from Dave as possible and left him crying. He beat me thoroughly and then dragged me to the toilet and flushed the tablets down one by one.

Not too long after that incident, he started to hit me, and warned that if I ever told anyone or tried to leave him he would kill me – and I believed him. By this time, I was expecting my second child.

Like many abusers – as I later learned – they isolate their victims. Suli refused to let me have friends; he would tell me that they would mislead me.

My second pregnancy was a very difficult one. I wasn't very well and I was also being beaten up on a regular basis by Suli. Eventually and miraculously, I gave birth to a beautiful baby girl, Angel.

Life became increasingly difficult for me after this. The beatings didn't stop and I now had two babies who were more like twins and very demanding; there was only about 17 months between them. If I wasn't feeding one, I would be changing the other's nappy. There was always something to do. I hardly had time to rest or just time on my own.

Worse still, by this time, I had no say in anything. Suli would not allow it. Sex? That happened whenever Suli wanted it to happen. I cannot describe to you how I felt during the act. My heart broke many times over. What kept me going was the fact that I had two beautiful children whom I had to look after and both of whom I loved very, very much.

An added problem was that I was not even allowed to look for a job as Suli was very possessive. You wonder why I would want go to work with two little children.

Well, as you might know, babies can be very expensive and Suli did not provide all the time or adequately.

At the end of the month when he was paid his wages, because he smoked and drank, he would 'disappear' for two or three days, I would not know where he is. On his return, he would have no money left to give to me. And if I asked where he had been, he would shout at me, asking who do I think I am to ask him such a question and would beat me yet again.

One day Linda, my eldest sister, who was still abroad at the time, got to know the seriousness of my situation. She was very upset and straight away wrote a letter to Suli telling him that he had to let me go out to find work and also that he should stop beating me. The letter provided some respite; he allowed me to look for a job but unfortunately did not stop beating me. Thank goodness I got a job as a temporary teacher at a Primary School.

What did I do to try and stop Suli from abusing me the way he did? In those days, there wasn't much help – at least not in the way that I needed it. I was close to some members of Suli's family. In fact, one of them, his aunty and Nora, her daughter did not live too far away from me. So when I could, I would go over to their house for refuge. I could not sleep there but I could tell aunty what was happening. She would get Suli to come, lock me in a room so that he could not reach me to hurt me and speak to him sternly. It made no difference.

When we get home, he would beat me just because I had gone to tell someone that he was abusing me. Members of his family loved me very much. They kept telling Suli to treat me right because I was a good person. Suli did not listen.

My family, whom I was not very close to and whom I felt I had disgraced by being 'damaged' could not help me much either. I do not know if they wanted to take action to stop me from being abused; all I know is that I was alone and there was no help for me.

I was not only physically abused; I was emotionally and mentally severely abused by Suli. I am sure you are wondering, why I did not pack up, take my children and run away. Remember, I was a child of war, I went to war, I did not have mummy or daddy. I had my grandmother who brought me up until I went to war at the age of 15. I practically brought myself up. What does a 15 year old know, anyway?

When I got back from war, I went to school, my first proper school but all I had going for me was a determination, a grit and guts that I was going to make something of myself in life. I wanted to make my mum proud of me. So when it came to emotions, I was far removed. I was not emotionally mature or developed enough to know what to do in situations like the one I found myself in.

It seemed to me that it was better being beaten physically by Suli than to hear the words he constantly spoke at me. That was all I knew. Even though I tried to get help, there was no help anywhere. Some of the demeaning words that Suli would say to me are:

"You are ugly!"

"You are nothing without me, I will say what and how about your life!"

"What kind of man would even look at you the way that you are?"

"You are so useless!"

"Other women are better than you."

"You have no discretion; you just go about telling people things that are not true."

"Do as I say or else…"

If we were out in public and men were looking at me, he would give me a warning look. Once we were out and about, We came across one of my friends, a young man who was in my boarding school and I had not seen him for a very long time, he excitedly greeted me saying, 'How are you? Where have you been keeping your beautiful self?" I said, 'I have been around only I have children now." Dave my son was with me. "Oh are you married?" I looked down and said, 'No, not really." My voice was very low.

All this time, Suli was glaring at me and my school mate noticed so he lowered his voice and asked, "So, where do you live?" By this time, I could hardly carry on with the conversation with Suli glaring at me the way he was.

When we got home that day, Suli went to town with words that cut deep. He said, "So, why did you tell him you were not married? You were making yourself available, weren't you? "Let me tell you, no one is interested in you. You are not beautiful and you are not worth it.

So forget whatever you thought you were going to do."

I was not married to Suli as at the time Beautiful, my second child, was born because according to my tradition and culture, I could not be pregnant when the families meet to discuss the dowry. That in itself was a disgrace to my family and to me.

I used to think it was my entire fault. I would clean, cook, do the best that I could and yet it seemed to Suli that nothing I did was good enough. If I talked to him or asked a question just so that I could make sure I got it right, he would shout at me and beat me. If I did not speak to him just to make sure that I did not annoy him, he would get annoyed and beat me. I could not win.

When he knew he had beaten me up really bad, he would go out and buy me a present; once he bought me a dress, brought it home and gave it to me. He would say something like this, 'I have bought you a present, here. I am sorry I beat you the way I did but it is your fault. If you behave yourself and be a good girl, I will not beat you, OK.'

After incidents like that, I would think he was really sorry and he would not beat me again but that was not the case. He beat me whenever he chose. The presents were probably just to make him feel better, not me – because I didn't feel any better.

Before I knew it I was pregnant again. This time I felt like this was the end of my life. I didn't think I could survive another pregnancy. How much more could I take? Things were going bad to worse; I was in despair. How could I carry another child for nine months again? How was I to tell my family that I was pregnant again? I had disgraced them enough.

After another 'long' pregnancy I gave birth to a beautiful baby boy, Shepherd. But let me tell you what happened when I was eight months pregnant with Shepherd, my third child and second son. I was planning for the birth when I asked Suli for money to start to purchase what I would need. It was about 1 or 2am in the middle of the night. It was late.

He said he did not have money and I should not ask him again. I told him he cannot do that because I needed the money and I had to prepare for the birth. Before I knew it, Suli had blown his top. He began beating me. He had particular instruments he used to beat me; sometimes he would use the iron rod which we put in fire to mould things or he would use an electric extension cable or his belt. As he punched me with his fists, he left me in the living room to go get his belt which is what he really wanted to use this time to beat me.

As he left the room, usually I would just stay put awaiting my beating, but this time, at eight months pregnant, something rose up on the inside of me and I ran out of the house. I fled down the long road ahead of me hoping that I would reach the turn in the road before he came out looking for me and so he would not know where I had gone. But before I reached the turn in the road, he had come out of the house, saw me and started chasing me. I reached an alleyway and ran into it. In the alleyway was a trench, a ditch or some would call it a gutter in which dirty water ran. I jumped into this trench and hid my swollen body as best I could.

I heard Suli come running. When he got to the alleyway, I could hear him breathing heavily. He must have been looking around wondering where I had gone. He left but I didn't know. I was too scared to peep out and see although I could not hear the heavy breathing anymore after a time. I did not know when he left so I stayed in the trench for another 30 minutes or so.

I came out slowly; unsure as to whether Suli was standing there waiting for me. .When I came out of the trench and did not see Suli, I started running again. I did not know where I was going but I wanted to get as far away from Suli as I could. Suddenly, I heard some commotion behind me. I looked back and noticed a group of young men.

Whenever I ran, they ran. Whenever I walked because I was tired of running, they would walk too. This carried on until I realised that they were following me and trying to catch me.

I was afraid. It was probably 3am in the middle of the night, and here I was, an unmarried pregnant mother carrying an 8 month old pregnancy escaping from the abusive father of her children, with a swollen face where he had used his fist to hit me before going to get his belt.

Where was I going?

Where could I go?

I kept running and walking and so did the young men behind me.

As I ran, I noticed lights were off in the houses I went past; I noticed there was only one house with lights on. I ran to its door and started banging on it crying and shouting for someone to please help me because my life was in danger. A few minutes later, a woman came to the window, parted the curtains and saw me with my swollen face and swollen belly. She opened the door, let me in and locked it behind me.

I began crying saying some men were chasing after me and she should please not let them into her house in case they would come there.

She assured me that they would not come to her house and put a blanket around me. She allowed me to spend the night there in her house.

Next morning, I left and made the very long walk back home. Suli had left for work by the time I got home. On his return, he had bought me yet another gift to say yet another 'sorry.' By this time, I did not care.

So many times during this period I would think that if my father had still been alive that he would have taken me out of this horrible situation that I had found myself. My life was in a mess; most of my ex-school mates were now either at university or college, and yet here I was, stuck in an abusive relationship with no way of getting out, all the while still having children for my abuser.

Sometimes it would feel like a bad dream, or worse still, a nightmare, and I prayed that I would wake up to find that it was just that a really bad dream. Unfortunately this was no nightmare – this was real: I had three children for a man I was not married to and I was in an abusive relationship; how much worse could anyone's life be?

There were times when I would lie awake at night praying for dawn because the darkness scared me so much. It even seemed that the longest times of the day were at night. Till today, I am still terrified of the dark.

After I had Shepherd, I began to desperately look for a permanent job as I had to provide for my children. By this time Suli had defaulted on paying the rent and we had been evicted by the landlord. We went to live in a house with my sister, Linda had bought for my mum although she was still abroad with my sister. I explained to my family that it was not a good idea for Suli will still be abusing me and I do not want my mum to see that. But, I guess my family did not realise the seriousness of my situation so we moved in and so did my grandmother from the village.

My job hunting was not going so good either as I did not have much experience in any industry apart from teaching, and by this time I had also lost confidence in myself and so I was not doing very well at interviews too.

One night I had a dream that my grandmother was on top of a building and she was calling my name at the top of her voice. I was walking on the pavement below with so many people in a busy town. I thought she was going to give up, but she kept calling me, and didn't stop until I decided to go up there and tell how embarrassed I felt. So I made my way upstairs, although when I reached the top I found a nice

office and an empty chair, but no grandmother.
I was still admiring the office when I woke up.

The following morning I told my grandmother
about my dream before I went out job hunting.
My grandmother was actually a very strong
Christian and after I told her what happened
she got out her Bible, read a passage in the
Bible, I cannot remember which it was and
prayed for me. She told me that it was a good
dream and that God had a job in store for me. I
had such a long day on this particular day after
my final interview and I felt like giving up
because I did not think I did well in any of
them.

On my way home I saw a very tall building
which was called Charter House, by this time I
had completely forgotten about my dream. I
went straight to the security guard and asked if
he knew if any of the companies in the building
were recruiting. He looked me up and down as

if I had asked him a million-dollar question. After a short silence he replied, "Not that I know of." He then asked me what type of job I was after and I told him that any kind of job would do. He apologised and said that he could not help me. I thanked him and wished him well anyway.

Just as I turned to leave, the security guard (I later learned that his name was Mr Sithole) called me back and said, "I heard that the law firm on the 8th floor was looking for a receptionist." He told me to go up to the 8th floor to Sansole & Senda where they would tell me the rest. Well, you can imagine how I felt! I thanked Mr Sithole profusely for his help and went up the lift.

Nervous as I was, when I got to the 8th floor I went straight to the receptionist to inquire about the supposed role, but she denied knowledge of the position. I then asked if I could see her manager – from the look on Mr Sithole's face downstairs I knew that something must be available and I hoped her manager might know more. I also remembered that even he – Mr Sithole – had at first told me that there were no positions. I knew that the receptionist was doing the same thing. I could see it in her eyes that she was not telling me the truth.

She went to call her manager but came back with news that he was very busy with a client, adding that he might be a while. I told her I did not mind waiting, and so I waited. It was over an hour before she called me back to the desk. The manager, Mr Ndlovu, was ready to see me. I went into his office as directed by the receptionist; he greeted me and offered me a seat. He began by asking me questions that had nothing to do with the job. I answered every question truthfully. For some reason, unlike all the other interviews, I seemed to have regained my confidence and felt much more at ease to answer all of his questions.

Eventually, he asked why I thought I could do the job as a receptionist when I had no previous experience. I told him that I knew all I needed was for someone to give me a chance and I would do my best in whatever role I was given. He asked me numerous questions about my family life; about my children and home. I could see that he was genuinely interested the way he asked me these questions. All this time I did not know that this was the actual interview, but that must have been a good thing because if I had known, I probably would have messed it all up. He probably was not going to give me another chance.

He showed me a pile of applications from other candidates who had applied for the same job; most of them had the experience and qualifications needed for the post. I thought to myself, why would he even consider me at all, I thought this was too good to be true.

His next question surprised me.

"If I were to offer you the job when would you be able to start?"

"As soon as possible, or as soon as you need me; I can start now really", I answered.

"Sure, Mr Ndlovu; tomorrow would not be a problem." I was excited!

"That's it then. You start tomorrow at 9am. Report to my office, your contract will be ready then."

I could not believe my ears! I just got offered a job. For about a minute I sat there dumb-struck, not being able to move or say anything.

"You got the job, happy now? If you don't mind please leave now as my next appointment has just arrived. I will see you tomorrow" Mr Ndlovu said

I came back to myself and thanked him profusely. "Thank you sir, thank you! Yes, I will see you tomorrow at 9am".

As I left his office I walked past the receptionist who had said there were no jobs going and therefore no reason to wait. I waved at her and said that I'd see her tomorrow. She looked at me as if I were mad. As I was leaving I remembered my dream and I thought to myself – there must be someone up there who cares about me.

When I got home I broke the news to my children, although they still very little, I spoke to them a whole lot because somehow I knew that they would understand. They were happy when I was happy and this time, they knew I was very happy. I also told my grandmother, who said to me, "Did I not tell you that God had a job just for you?" I was so happy.

The following day I wore one of my old suits, which really was the best one I had, to my first day at work. When I got to work I got to meet all the lawyers and barristers, as well as all the other staff members, and everyone gave me a warm welcome.

It was a very big law firm and one receptionist could not handle the number of calls and clients that came through the door. In fact, in the past there had been three receptionists but two had left and now I was to be the second.

The next three months were crucial for me as I was on probation and I had to make sure I impressed my employer. At the end of my probation period, I was made a permanent member of staff. All my bosses were very pleased with my work. Some said to me that for someone who has never worked in an office before I was quite good. Thank goodness I was good at something at least. I worked for this firm for three years until I eventually came to England.

Looking back, it was my place of refuge during the day. When the day ended the only thing I looked forward to; was seeing my babies. But on the other hand, things were getting worse and worse.

One Day at a Time!

Something major happened by the time I had worked for the firm for two years; my mum finally came back from England. I had not seen her for six years. I was glad to have her back and I was not so glad at the same time. Because I knew it would be a matter of time before she could experience in full technical colour the seriousness and nature of the kind of life I was living. I did not want that nor did I look forward to it.

One day after work, I was running a bit late getting back home due to transportation problems. A friend of mine, James, drove past me waiting at the bus stop and stopped to ask if I needed a lift home.

I thought to myself that it would be wiser to get a lift home from James than to be any later getting home because I knew Suli would be really angry with me if I get home any later. Considering how he reacted to one of my male friends whom we met in the market place, as I stated earlier, it seemed to be the lesser of two evils. As we pulled into my mother's house, Suli came out of the house yelling and demanding answers.

"Who is this?" referring to my friend.

"Why are you in his car?"

"How do you know him?"

He looked like he might start a fight with James.

My body started to shake with fear. I knew that as soon as James drove off he was going to deal with me very harshly. I did not know what to expect but I knew it would only be more abuse, more of the same. I was so terrified. I wished the earth could have swallowed me up right there, a wish I have had many times before. Finally, after a big argument my friend drove off. Suli came straight at me like a roaring lion and grabbed me with his strong clumsy hands.

"You, come here now! I will show you who I am today!"

I started to plead for his mercy, as I always do, begging him not to beat me up.

I screamed. I begged him over and over again, but nothing would make him stop. That night was one of the worst nights of my life.

What was even more painful, more than the physical pain, was that all this was happening in front of my children, my sister, my mother and my grandmother, although she was locked up in my mum's bedroom; my mum had asked her to go there, these were the most important people in my life.

My children were crying out 'Mama lo!' A cry from the depths of their heart when something is wrong. As for my mother, I cannot imagine the pain, the agony of what she was going through as a parent, watching her daughter being beaten up. I believe this would be any mother's nightmare.

I guess Suli was no longer bothered about my mother's presence; it seemed to me that he believed that he owned me. This particular night was one of the worst and I had to be taken to the hospital by the time he was done with me. I must have fainted, because the next thing I remember was waking up in a pool of water. In some parts of Africa, including my country, if you faint they believe that pouring cold water over you would revive you.

When the doctors examined me they found out I had a fracture on the side of my head. I would also have to undergo an operation on my right eye as I had a blood clot inside. An appointment was made for two days later. I was terrified as I had never had an operation before. I was so scared of losing my eye, my life – everything was so overwhelming at this point.

The day for my surgery came and one of my sisters took me to Hospital. When we got there I was given a form to fill out which my sister signed to give consent for the operation. I was then taken in to the theatre where the operation would take place. The doctor came in and introduced himself. "I am Dr Dlamini and I am the anaesthetist. Now could you please count up to ten for me?" I never reached ten and my next memory was after the operation; it had been successful, thank God.

In the two days after the operation I could not go to work as I still sore, especially on my face,

I had bruises around my eyes. I was off work for about one week. At this stage my confidence as a woman and as a person were completely stripped away. I felt so insecure, so ashamed, the feeling of 'nothingness' was so overwhelming. The sense of worthlessness that I had, was almost overpowering.

This is why I have written this book so that all men and women will know that we are all precious in the eyes of God. None of us is less, I AM NOT LESS, and nobody has a right to make any human being feel the way I did.

After the operation Dr Dlamini wanted to have a word with my sister and I. His first question to me was frank and straight to the point. "Tell me something, are you married to the person who is beating you up?" I answered that I was not. His next question was, "Why then are you staying with him?" I said that it was because of my three children, I cannot just leave them.

The next thing Dr Dlamini said left me thinking. "Can you not see that it is a miracle that you are alive? This man could have killed you.

Which brings me to a question I would like to ask your sister, assuming she is your blood sister? If so, why are you letting her stay with this man? Can't you see that one day this man will kill her?" He went on to say, "If the reason for staying is because of your children, is that not even more reason to leave now while you are alive, then at least you can take your children. If you die, then tell me what will happen to your children?"

Looking back, I believe that Dr Dlamini was an Angel sent by God, because after that conversation I knew that I had to do something with or without my family's support.
Unknown to me, my mother was feeling the same. She knew that my life could not

continue the way things were. At this time Suli continued to threaten me, saying that he was going to kill me. With all this happening all that was in my heart was so much hatred, so much pain.

Meanwhile, the news had travelled to England where my eldest sister, Linda, had settled with her family. Between her and my mother they agreed that it was high time to rescue me from the situation that I was in. So my sister arranged a ticket for me to fly to England.

Desperate Times Call for Desperate Measures

The ticket was arranged through a travel agent. It had to be kept a complete secret; we could not reveal anything about my upcoming trip to Suli until my eldest brother, Gideon had spoken to him. Remember, even up until now Lobola (Dowry), or wedding plans could not be discussed with the Suli's family. My brother had made this clear to them and to Suli.

Therefore, by rights, I still belonged to my family. Suli had no rights over me even though I had given birth to three children for him.

A few weeks after my family decided to rescue me from this situation, appropriate arrangements which had been made went ahead and my ticket was purchased. The travel agent had been warned not send any information about my travel arrangements or itinerary to my home address and instead to let us know when we could come and pick it up from their offices. The plan was to pick it up on the day of my travel. Sadly the opposite was done. Suli picked me up from work one day, and as we got home the baby sitter told me of a letter that had arrived for me.

"Auntie; a letter came for you", she said. I responded by asking her to bear with me so I could put my bags down and say hello to my children after a long day at work.

Suli demanded to see the letter. Unknown to me, my younger sister, Lucie had taken the letter as soon as she realised that it was from the travel agent. She knew that Suli was not to know until Gideon had spoken to him about me leaving the country. We all knew that if Suli found out about it beforehand, he was bound to hit the roof and sabotage the whole thing. He had always told me that I could never escape from him; he would find me and kill me if I tried.

It was probably intuition, but throughout that day into the night, I felt like something was wrong. I could not put my finger on it and I suppressed the feeling while I was at work. But the feeling did not go away when Suli picked me up from work and we came home.

My attention was brought back into the room as Suli continued to demand where the letter was, from the baby sitter. The letter was nowhere to be found.

Suli turned to me. "Where is the letter?" he asked me.

I replied by reminding him that we had both just got home, I had no idea where this letter was or who it was from, or what it looked like.

After a good search of the house, the baby sitter herself was getting scared as she could see where this was heading to.

He turned to me and asked again, "Surely you must know who wrote you a letter?" I replied, repeating that I had no idea where the letter was.

Fear had begun to overwhelm me because I knew what was coming. If I knew where the letter was, I would have given it to him right at that moment.

However, the dreadful feeling that overwhelmed me already just increased in intensity as Suli became angrier and angrier. By this time everyone in the house was looking for this letter, including my mother. He started to roll up his sleeves and I knew he was getting ready to hit me. He grabbed me violently on my upper arm and demanded that I tell him where the letter was.

At this point my mother intervened, pleading with him not to start the beatings again. My children were in the corner crying. Everyone in the house knew what was about to happen.

My mother pleaded with him again, and then tried to get in between us. He grabbed my mother by both her arms and threw her across the room. My mother landed on the floor. I could not bear it. I would rather he had done that to me, than to my mum. Then he took me to the bedroom and locked the room with a cloth hanger.   That night he beat me up so badly.   At the start I was crying, pleading for help and begging him to stop, until I could not cry anymore.

That night he concluded his 'abusive session' with more threats.   He warned that he was watching my every move, and should I even try to leave him he would surely kill me.   I had heard him say this many times before and I knew Suli would do exactly that.

The following day, I could not go to work.   I had red eyes and my entire body hurt.   This time, I was not the only one in pain.   My mother was distraught and she was also physically ill.

My mother and I were resting under a mango tree in the garden when my sister Lucie came to sit with us.   She told me how much she loved me and how sorry she was about everything that happened last night.   I did not understand what she was on about but then she took out a letter – the missing letter.   She admitted that she had hidden it because she knew that if Suli had found out about the trip, it would have been the end of me.   I would never have been able to escape from him.

My brother, Gideon called a meeting with Suli, his family and mine.   Personally I was terrified; I did not know how this was going to work out. All I knew was that I believed Suli's threats wholeheartedly.

My brother announced to Suli's family, speaking as the father of our house.
"As you know, Fikelephi is still our daughter, by law, by tradition and by culture, because you are not married yet.   This meeting is not to ask for permission but rather to inform you that we are sending Fikelephi abroad to study. When you two met she was studying, and so we

are sending her back to school to finish her education."

There was a long, heavy silence in the room, during which time I was shaking like a leaf, as you can imagine. I was sat next to my mother and squeezed her hand so tight I might have broken it.

Mean while Suli was sweating; I could see his forehead. My brother did not give him much of a choice or ask for his opinion. His representative took a deep breath. Suli looked at me out of the corner of his eye. I could see the eyes spitting fire; if looks could kill I would have died there and then.

I was even more terrified.

After a while, his representative responded. He asked how long I would be gone for. My brother's response, "As long as the course lasted."

I can't remember the rest of the conversation. All I remember is my mother and I holding on to each other tightly.

This meeting took place three days before I was scheduled to travel. Those three days felt like a century.

Fike & Her Children

CHAPTER 4

Leaving My Children Behind

Any parent would agree with me that leaving your children behind is not an easy task, especially with all that we had been through. My heart was torn but my mind was made up. I was very determined to make it, and I would come back for them as soon as I was on my feet.   This option was definitely better than being six feet under, in the grave.   It made sense to escape while I still had breath in me, than to die in this situation.

Those three days were the hardest for me.   I could not eat or sleep and I had stomach pains. I constantly felt like using the toilet, but it was just a feeling borne out of how nervous I was. This was almost surreal to me. I was restless; counting down each hour until I left the country.   Thinking of my children, I kept praying that if only I could make it – for their sakes – that would be a miracle.

Meanwhile, I still had to go to work. When my employers knew that I was leaving, they were concerned that they would not be able to get someone who worked just as well as I did. I suggested that my junior sister, Lucie would be a great replacement because we had similar attitudes to work. They agreed and I promised to train her before I left.

I trained Lucie and within a week, she knew exactly how things worked in the law firm. She was a very fast learner although she had only just finished her O levels and all she had was a reference from the principal of her school.

The day came and I was still alive; well, just. Suli was still threatening as usual, although this time I was the one assuring him that I had no intention of leaving him. I promised that I would come straight back home as soon as my studies were over.

The day finally came. I could barely sleep as there was a big battle going on in my mind. Remember that by this point, not only did I feel that I was a failure; I felt I had also disgraced the family, my children, and myself. All my peers from school were doing well; however, my life was a completely different story.

I knew this day would change my life forever.

My biggest concern, in fact my only one, was that I could not see how I was going to be reunited with my children. Would Suli allow them to come to me? Now you see, as much as Suli abused me, he loved his children very much and was very protective of them. I knew he would probably never let them go but somehow I was hopeful. I don't know how or why but something was telling me not to worry, 'One day you will see them, you will be reunited again'.

Somebody Pinch Me! Am I Dreaming?

The long awaited day was finally here. Today I would fly to England, not knowing what it was going to be like or who I was going to meet. I was determined to spend the remaining time I had with my children, assuring them that I was coming back for them as soon as I was settled and could provide for them. Dave was five, Beautiful was four and Shepherd was three years old when I left.

Now that the day had finally arrived, I found that as I got ready to leave I had mixed feelings. The most difficult thing would be to say goodbye to my children. Lucie and her husband-to-be drove with my children, Suli insisted on taking me in his car. As I got into the car I was shaking like a leaf, not knowing if I would make it to the airport, much less England. We were the only two in his car.

Lucie was quite concerned when Suli insisted that he will take me to the airport. So, they pretended to go ahead of us with the children to the airport but then turned around and drove behind Suli's car all the way to the airport just to make sure I arrived there.

As we set off, I believed all the other cars went ahead of us. Ten minutes before we reached the airport, he stopped the car and told me there was a problem with the car. He opened the car bonnet. I knew that that was the end of me. I was sure that he would make me miss my plane; that he would never let me go.

Fear again, began to overwhelm me. Suddenly, a car pulled up behind ours. I looked back and it was Lucie, my younger sister and her husband-to-be; they had been driving behind us as they had suspected that he must have had an ulterior motive. Her fiancé asked what was wrong with the car and upon restarting it, it turned out there was nothing wrong with the car. Meanwhile, my sister took me into their car and I rode with them for the rest of the way. That was a narrow escape.

When we got to the airport, the last call was being made for my flight and my name was being announced; I was the only passenger who was not yet on the plane.

I'm not sure if you've ever felt so nervous where you feel like going to the bathroom but you can't because your stomach hurts? I was shaking all the way through the flight. It was as though I was dreaming. I don't remember hearing a word of what the airhostess was talking about – in the event of a fire, the gas mask, and all the rest. Mind you, to add to my nervousness, this was my very first time on a plane. For the next ten hours I set there on the plane, pinching myself to make sure I was not dreaming.

We arrived in the early hours of the next morning at Heathrow Airport in the United Kingdom where my eldest sister, Linda was waiting to receive me. I was crying and sobbing with joy that I had actually escaped. Linda kept asking me how the children were and how I was. She had some cards which had been sent to me from other friends. I had finally escaped from the lion's den as it were and I was free.

Suli & The Children Move House

While I was still working at the Solicitors firm, there were houses being planned and built and my firm was hired to deal with the conveyance.
I was able to buy one of these houses even before it was actually built. I was allocated one of them. After I left, the houses were built and ready for occupation.

It became apparent before then that Suli could no longer live in my mother's house. So it was just right that soon after I travelled to the UK, Suli and the children were able to move to my newly acquired, newly built house. The family had allowed Suli's younger sister to come live with Suli and I while I was still in South Africa. So when it was time to move, he moved with the children and his younger sister, Mabel, into my house. Mabel helped with the children but Suli also hired a house maid who also took care of the children; she was a wonderful girl.

Now, my children lived about an hour away from my mum. However, mum was able to visit with them often. As well as Yasmin who used to take them away during school holidays and kept a strict eye on how they were doing as she kept me updated constantly. Yasmin was the one I planned their birthday celebrations with. She was the one who could tell me what each of the children was currently interested in and I would go ahead, purchase it and post over as their gifts from me.

She would give me as precise an account of how the birthday celebrations went whenever their birthdays came round. In spite of Suli's abusive behaviour, he demonstrated that he loved the children. After I left, he stepped up and provided money for them; he no longer travelled for days although that did not stop him being abusive towards Mercy. I took care to ensure that my experiences with Suli did not affect my children. I made a point of always telling them I loved them and their Dad loved them too.

CHAPTER 5

New Day, New Beginnings

I arrived at my sister's house to meet my nephew and two nieces who were pleased to see me. There were also a few family friends who were looking forward to seeing me, as they had heard a lot about my predicament.

The first few nights, I hardly slept, because Linda had so much to ask me. These were all very exciting times for me.

What hurt in the midst of all the excitement was that quite a few of my sister's friends knew the details of my predicament and gossiped about it.

Also, as time went on, I noticed that one of my nieces, the younger one was still a baby; and nephew were not allowed to come near me because they were told that I will be a bad influence on them even though my niece loved me very much; I had taken care of her when she was little before they came to England. This upset me a great deal.

My sister did not understand why I was still so timid and fearful even though I had left the situation behind. She wondered what my problem was, after all she had brought me all the way to England and all I did was cry and cry everyday at the slightest upset. I couldn't explain it to her. I hardly could understand it myself. All I knew was that I was full of fear and I did not know what to do about it.

Two weeks after I arrived in the UK, my brother-in-law who had connections with the office of the High Commission had gone ahead to introduce me in absentia to those who could offer me a job. With that he was informed of a vacancy for the position of Information Officer in their offices This was wonderful news for me when I was told.

I was encouraged to apply, which I did, and the following week I got a letter calling me in for an interview. Coming from a place where I was not allowed to get a job to a place where a job seemed to be waiting for me. Plus, getting a job would mean that I could continue to provide for my children back home and I would also be able to pay my mother back the money she had lent me to buy my ticket.

This interview was very different. There were two people on the panel. After a lot of grilling, I was informed that I had gotten the job. However, there was no way I could start working until the Organisation was able to sort out my visa and work permit. At this stage, the administrator requested for my passport and identity card and all the other paper work which were taken to the Home Office for processing.

Little did I know what this would mean for me, I went back to my sister's house after the interview. A few weeks after the interview, it became obvious that I needed to find another job while I waited for the High Commission to sort out my papers with the Home Office.

During this time, even though I was physically away from my abuser, mentally I was still chained. I still felt very delicate, very tender, especially as the nightmares continued. It was clear to anyone who saw me that I had been traumatised; I was very depressed, timid, with no self-confidence whatsoever. I found it hard to open up to anyone. I was scared of the dark. I could still hear Suli's words saying, "You are nothing, you are ugly, and you will never amount to anything. Do not even try to leave me, as I will make sure I find you and kill you with my bare hands."

If you hear something over and over again you end up believing it's true. Do you see how I was still in my prison, even though physically I was out?

At night I would cry my eyes out, reliving every detail, every slap, every punch in my mind.

I desperately missed my children, the pain was intense! The worst thing was that there was nothing I could do about the situation. I had to hope for the best and continued taking one day at a time. It was also challenging because my siblings (my other older sister, Charis was also living with Linda; she had come down to the UK when my mum travelled back) both of them could not understand what the problem was since I was not with Suli anymore.

I had to snap out of this nightmare. I had to find a job, and fast. It had become obvious that it was going to take longer than I thought for the Home Office to process my visa and work permit.

So one day I went into town with my sister Linda, searching for a job.   I went to five different Employment Agencies but only two of these cared to listen.   Remember I had no documents to identify myself because all my papers were at the Home Office.   I was honest with the agencies and told them about the position I was due to occupy at the Organisation's office once my pending visa application had been approved by the Home Office.

One of the two agencies offered me a job in a factory.   It was hard work, with long days from 5:00am until 4:00pm.This went on for about six months.   During this time I was able to send money back home to pay back my ticket money to my mum and also provide for my children.

Yet Another Twist

After six months however, the agency began to demand to see my documents, they wanted my visa and my National Insurance number.   I could not meet these demands as I was still waiting for my papers to be returned from the Home Office. I recall after one long shift, my manager called me over and informed me that they could not keep me at the factory any longer unless I fulfilled their requirements. Once I had brought in my paperwork they would be happy to have me back at work, he said. I begged him to allow me to stay. Work was the only thing that kept me going during the day, until night fell when the nightmares would continue. I begged and begged but the answer was the same. I had to stop working at the factory. Rejection was painful, but then again, that was the story of my life so far. Nobody wanted to know.

I took this rejection personally.

The Last Straw

A few months later there was still no news from the Home Office. One day, I met with a Sangoma man (that is, a witch doctor) who asked me to have a consultation with him. Reluctantly, I agreed.

The Sangoma man started by telling me that a man in my life had done Voodoo or witchcraft on me (he was referring to Suli). He told me that I was like a person who was locked in a dark room and the keys had been lost. He warned that the spirit told him that I would never get married, would never get a job; the curses went on and on. What was new, I asked myself. I was convinced that none of these will happen to me anyway – that I certainly wouldn't get married and neither would I get a job.

I asked the Sangoma man what I had to do to change my situation.

His response: I had to pay the spirits £200.

I was shocked to hear this as the Sangoma man himself had just confirmed that my life was written off. Where would I get the money from, I asked him.

He replied, saying that sadly his hands were tied, he could not 'fix' me.

For me that was the last straw. I told myself that enough was enough; I was not going to buy my life from anyone. All the while, the nightmares continued and my depression intensified. The following morning I went to town, back to those two employment agencies, to beg for a job. I had debts to pay off and three children to take care of.

I rang one of the agencies from a public phone box and spoke to Walter, the manager, who said to me, deliberately and slowly, "There is no position for you unless you sort out your visa and National Insurance number. Please do not call this office again." After which, he hung up the phone on me. I had been waiting in line for a long time to use the phone only to receive this very disappointing reply. That was it; I had had enough!

Turning Point

At this point I lost it in the phone box. I began to cry uncontrollably. I was in despair. I started screaming and shouting out words...to something or someone, I did not know neither did I care. Others were on the queue outside the phone box waiting to use it and had begun to shout at me to get out, because they could see that I had hung up the phone. But I did not care about that either. They seemed to have all they needed and I didn't; that was all I cared about.

I was angry at my father.
'Why did you die and leave me behind in this cruel world? Why was it that my grandmother was the only one who really loved me and cared for me during my childhood, the one who brought me up?' I felt this sudden urge to talk to her, there and then. Then it dawned on me: both my father and my grandmother were dead. Grandmother had died after I gave birth to

Shepherd; he was just over a year old. I missed her so much.

Then I remembered that she used to tell me about God.

She used to tell me that God was the Alpha and Omega, the beginning and the end of everything. I remembered she told me that He created the heavens and the earth and that He had the power over the entire world. She told me that He created me, and that He had a plan and purpose for my life. I didn't understand a lot of what she said then but I did remember her words.

So in that moment I lifted my face to the heavens and begged Him to take the life He had given me back. I had made a mess of my life. I told Him that I was sorry I had failed Him and I had failed my children. Surely, if he made me; he must be ashamed of me like everyone else was.

I told him I realised that I must have been a mistake and insisted He takes His life back. I was more than happy to assist Him if He didn't do it Himself; I was happy to take my own life. I really had lost it; I was fed up; I had had quite enough. There had to be a turning point here and now and I was screaming at this God to make this turning point a reality.

I Made A Vow

Finally, I said to this God my grandmother always told me about, that if there was any reason why He made me, if there was a reason for my existence I wanted to know urgently. I told Him I was going to wait for three days for a sign, and if not, I would take my life.

My grandmother had told me He was bigger than everyone and could speak to people's hearts. And this was the sign I wanted, I asked Him to speak to Walter, the manager of the employment agency and convince him to give me the job. I assured God that if I did not see this sign then that would be my answer that it was OK by Him for me to take my life. To be honest, this was not so much about the job, but more about me knowing that He would hear me and answer me.

Why was this important?
Because my grandmother would dance about the house telling me how she had asked God for something and He had heard and answered her.
Well, it was either He answered only my grandmother or He would answer me too.
I was going to find out one way or another.

It was my ultimatum. I had to know urgently or this was going to be the end?

I left the phone box feeling lighter. I felt as though I had finally spoken to the person who was responsible for my existence.

Of course you can imagine, my eyes were swollen from crying and I had mucus coming out from my nostrils. I was a right mess. But did I care about my appearance as I stepped out of the box? No, not at all. All I cared about right then was whether God would answer me and speak to Walter as I had asked or I was going to take my life. I had it all planned. I would go to the train station; it would be easy, just stand on the track and wait for the train to run me over.

It would be quick too. When I got back to my sister's house my eyes were still swollen from crying. But my mind was made up.

CHAPTER 6

God Answers

Day one: I was numb. All I needed to do was figure out what I would say to my three lovely children. For hours I pondered in my head what words I would use. I stayed in my room all day.

Day two: I pinched myself knowing that it was less than 48 hours before I would end my life or before I would hear from Walter.. My heart was beating fast, but still my mind was made up. I had started drafting a few letters, tearing several drafts and starting again. I could not die without saying goodbye to the people I loved, my children, my mum and my siblings – at least.

However, late in the afternoon of day two, a phone call came through. My nephew came running up the stairs to my room, calling "Auntie, auntie, phone call for you". I really didn't care who could be on the other side of the line; whoever they were this would be my last conversation with them.

Little did I know that this phone call would change my life:

"Hello", I said.

The person on the other end of the line was – yes, you guessed right, it was Walter, the employment agency manager.

"Fikelephi, this is Walter. I have something for you..."
As soon as I heard his name, I screamed.
"Please do not get carried away, it's only for three days..."
But I didn't care; God had actually heard me and answered me.
I knew then that He had heard me. I cried out to the heavens and He heard me. With less than a day to live or so I thought, He came

through for me and I still could not get my head round it. In my heart of hearts, I knew that He heard me and He had listened this disheartened woman, a woman who was in complete despair; who had brought disgrace to all around her.

I Pinch myself, I'm still alive

Day three: its 5:00am the mini bus came to fetch me and took five of us to Northampton Hospital, where I was to spend the next three days working as a seamstress, darning the hospital bed sheets using an industrial sewing machine. I found later, as Walter informed me that I was the only one on their books who had this experience and as they had never been hired by the hospital before, my lack of essential documents did not matter; as an agency they wanted the job from the hospital as it increased their profile. The four others who went with me were to assist me by folding the sheets and doing other odd jobs.

I was still in deep conversation with the Creator of Heaven and Earth (this was one of the ways my grandmother referred to Him when she spoke to me), I acknowledged that I knew He heard me, though I still wanted to know why He created me. As I had promised I would work hard, do whatever it takes to live the life He had created me for; all He had to do was to tell me what that was. I felt, surely if He saved me from killing myself by getting Walter to offer me this job then, my life has got to be worthwhile.

I knew that the new job offer was for three days only. But I told him that surely whatever he did to change Walter's mind, he will do again before the three days was up.

In the mini bus, I introduced myself to the four other colleagues who I would spend the next three days with; there were two women and two men. We arrived at the hospital and we were shown to the launderette and the sewing room. There were ten industrial sewing machines. We were then briefed on the task for the day and they asked how many of us could use the industrial sewing machine. As it turned out, I was the only one who could use these machines out of the five of us. I was given a machine while the others were assigned to folding the sheets. The job was very simple; we were to mend the hospital sheets. I had done Fashion and Fabrics at school for my 'O' Levels and had enjoyed sewing.

This love for sewing must have reflected in my work that day as everyone kept saying "Well done", and that I was doing great. I impressed my managers as well.

It had become my habit to think that everyone was just being polite because I had concluded that I was worthless and could do nothing right. But I was encouraged when at the end of the day, my new manager waved goodbye as I left and said she would see me tomorrow.

The following day I was picked up as usual but I noticed that my colleagues were not in the mini bus. When I got to work, I was told by my manager that they had called Walter from the agency to say that they did not need the five of us. It turned out that the other four had been dismissed and I was the only one they needed.

Now that was a surprise. 'Someone actually thinks I'm worth something', I thought to myself, 'They want me.' I kept talking to the Guy upstairs still throughout the day. To be honest, I was still shocked at how things were working out for me since having given my ultimatum. Maybe there was a God after all like grandmother said. I was surprised that He could not only speak to Walter, but to my new boss as well. Still I wondered what He would do next. Time was running out from where I was standing.

On the final day of the 'contract', as it were, the mini bus came to pick me up and took me to the hospital. A strange thing happened when I arrived at work. When I got to work, my new boss had her arms open wide and give me a big hug. I was hesitant; I did not know what to think. And I wasn't a touchy-feely person at all.

I thought to myself, "She must want something from me."
I could not think of any other reason why she would be so nice to me. Reluctantly I responded timidly to her gesture. After she hugged me she ushered me to my sewing machine.

During lunch time, a few of the workers attempted to make conversation with me, but sadly there was nobody home. I was in my own world, cloud-cuckoo-land you could call it. From time to time when I wasn't talking to the big Guy upstairs, I would join in their conversations.

Little did I know that my manager Kathy was a Christian. From the moment I walked into that hospital, God had spoken to her clearly about me. In her own words she said to me, "God told me that you were suicidal, it was an emergency and that I must pray for you. I was also to deliver a message to you, that God loves you and that's why He sent His Son Jesus to die for you on the cross. He also has a plan and purpose for your life."

Three days turned into a week, and then into two weeks. I had to keep pinching myself, and yes, I was still alive. I asked Him over and over again to tell me why He made me. I also thanked Him continuously for answering my prayer and showing me a sign. During this time, my boss was really doting on me and she started bringing me sandwiches for lunch. The first time she offered me a sandwich I refused, asking how much this was going to cost me? I certainly couldn't afford this. She assured me she made the packed lunch especially for me and wasn't expecting anything in return. I made a mental note to stay away from this old woman who I was certainly a bit mad. One day during lunch, as she handed me the packed lunch again, she said to me "God loves you Fikelephi."

I looked at her, at first with amusement, and then I completely broke down. She had touched a nerve. Before I knew it I was crying uncontrollably. I told her never to say such a thing to me again, because I considered it an insult.

I said to her, "If He loves me, why did He take away my grandmother just before I left Africa? The only person I felt that loved me? Why did He take away my father? Why is it that, right from the time I was born I felt I had to fight to survive?"

By this time I am sobbing on my boss's shoulders. I had completely forgotten about dignity.

I told her with all due respect that because she was old enough to be my mother, it would be better if she stayed away from me because my life was complicated and I seemed to hurt those who are close to me.

Something Strange Happened To Me

Despite my telling her to stay away, she insisted on talking to me, telling me that God had a plan and purpose for me. The plan He had for me was not meant to harm me, but to bring me to an expected end. I did not understand what she was talking about.

She said that she would not give up on me, as God Himself would never give up on me. She told me that my destiny was attached to hundreds of lives and that I had to pull through so they could pull through too. She confused me some more with all this 'Christianise.' What lives was I attached to? The only lives I felt I was responsible for were those of my three children who I was missing horrendously.

I did ask God to show me why He made me, and here was a total stranger, as old as my mum, telling me all these strange things which I did not comprehend. What was this Guy doing? I asked but did He not know that I have to understand as well?

She invited me to come to church with her on a Sunday, which I did but only after she had spent days and weeks speaking with me every day about God and His plans for me. The only reason I agreed to go to church with her was so that I could finally get rid of her. She didn't know this and I thought it would work.

But to make it even more difficult for me to get rid of her, she had told the agency not to send the mini bus to take me home anymore. She had begun to take me home in her car so that she could spend even more time with me.

She was true to her word; she planned not to give up on me.

There were numerous days when I would say to her that I was going to take a bus home even though it would have been a really long journey because the hospital was on the outskirts of town. She would refuse and I would argue with her trying to get my way.

I still did not know how to trust anyone. What with my sister's friends gossiping about me every day. I felt this will lead to more of the same. I just wanted to stay away. I was grateful for the job but that was all I wanted.

I cannot tell you today how difficult my boss found me, but I did make it quite difficult for her to get close to me. The packed lunches, the rides home, the talk about God having a plan and a purpose for me just made me want to go very far away from her. Did I succeed? Read on.

At her church, I met a few more people, mostly older than me, who I found out had been praying for me. They told me how my boss had told them all about me and how she had asked them to be praying for me. This was really different it was like living another kind of life. I thought they were weird people. They were all over me and I didn't get that. I was used to rejection and hearing how worthless I am. I was used to disgracing people and being told that I am a disgrace myself. My usual response was to hide away.

I was already in a box and these people seemed to be trying to get me out of the box or they were trying to enter my box. I did not want company, much less their own company. I just wanted to be left alone – alone was what I was used to.

Whenever I went to church with her, I would get hugs from the church members and greetings like, 'hello darling, it's so nice to see you at church today.'

Don't darling me was what was going on in my head.   After all everything seemed to be OK with them and it wasn't with me so I did not need this lovey-dovey stuff that they did.

But on a Tuesday, on our way home from work, when we got into the car, my boss looked at me. She had such a sincere expression on her face.   She   reminded   instantly   of   my grandmother in that moment. I wondered why she was looking at me that way.

She said she was not going to take me home but that there was a meeting she wanted me to attend; it was known as a 'home group.'

I asked her what this was and she explained that it was a church meeting but held in someone's home for just about an hour.

I was curious. I wanted to know what this was all about.   Plus, she looked suddenly quite different.   Her words were somewhat deeper than just the words she spoke.

But I got worried and asked if there will be a lot of people there.   She said no, it was just a few people and not as many as in the church and she assured me that she will be with me and I should not worry.

That day they prayed for me.   I told them about my children and they prayed for my three little angels too.

After we prayed, one of the ladies, Mrs Careen, asked me if I wanted to give my life to Christ.

By now, after I had been prayed for, something had happened on the inside of me which I could not explain.   I had begun to put two and two together.   I realised that everything they said to me that night was from the Bible, they had essentially repeated everything my grandmother used to tell me.

That night I said 'yes' to the big Guy upstairs when I said 'yes' to Mrs Careen.

I became born again.

That was what they called it after they led me to repeat a particular prayer after them.   They said my life was reconciled back to its Maker. In a nut shell they briefly explained to me the story about Adam and Eve.   In the beginning men had everything but God also gave specific instruction to them, that they should not eat a particular tree.   Sadly they gave into temptation and ate the very tree.   Because of what they did back then, it meant that each one.

Kathy along with Mr And Mrs Careen, led me in what I now understand is commonly referred to as the prayer of salvation.   I felt strangely different.   I had a certain peace in my heart for the first time in years. That night I slept through the night, until ten am. I cannot explain to you even today, how I did that.

Before that night, you could say I hardly sleep, some nights, I did not sleep because I would be thinking about my life, my children, memories would flood my mind of the painful days, minutes of being physically beaten. Other nights, I would have horrible nightmares that would wake me up making me unable to sleep anymore. So this night was a really special, unique and wonderful night.

Going Forward

Remember, for me it was a matter of life and death. I didn't have Jehovah Witnesses with Bibles in their hands; it was simply between the big Guy upstairs and I, that day in the telephone box. That was where I promised Him that I would tell the whole world about His goodness, if only He would turn my life around;

if only He would make my life better; if only He would do what my grandmother said He could do.

I remember clearly the two tormenting days of waiting – was I going to take my life or was that big Guy going to do what I asked?

When I woke up I realised I was late and I knew that the mini bus had left me behind. I would usually catch it at 6am each morning. The last thing I wanted to do was upset my new boss, and lose my new found opportunity. I ran downstairs and got ready as quickly as possible. As I was running around the house, getting myself ready, my nephew told me that there was a telephone message from my manager which he had written on a sheet. It said that I should not bother to come to work that day – I had been given the day off.

I couldn't believe it!

I was still feeling strange from last night and now I was being given a day off – what good thing could happen next?

It was Wednesday and now I could hardly wait for Sunday to tell Mrs Careen and even to go back to work on Thursday to tell Kathy that I actually slept through the night for the first time in years and how 'nice' I was feeling inside. I couldn't wait.

Kathy told me later that God had told her to give me space that day. When she told me this, I really did not think she was being serious. When did God start speaking to people, much less me? Oh well, it was good to have a day off all the same. I was ecstatic.

PUT LATER – PPL GET A NICE ALTAR CALL IN AN AIR CONDITIONED PALATIAL ROOM AND THEY GET TO COME OUT AND GET BORN AGAIN AND WE GET EXCITED FOR THEM.

WELL, I DID NOT HAVE THAT, ALL I HAD WAS A PHONE BOX, A HOME GROUP, A BOSS WHO WOULD NOT SHUT HER MOUTH AND LEAVE ME ALONE WHICH ALL LED TO MY FIRST FITFUL NIGHT OF SLEEP. FOR THIS I WANTED TO SCREAM WITH EXCITEMENT – IT DID NOT HAVE TO BE COMFORTABLE TO BE GOOD.

Meanwhile, Walter at the Recruitment Agency was taken aback; the hospital had initially said they needed me for only three days, but I was still there over three months later. He was making money. For me this was evidence that what my grandmother had taught me about God doing what you ask is true indeed.

My Children

CHAPTER 7

My Children

Meanwhile I had become an expert in being a Mummy overseas in more ways than one. Let me tell you about it.

I was able to send money over to my children; I would send it to my mum and she would disburse it as necessary towards the upkeep of my children. I became good friends with the principle of my children's school. I used to purchase phone cards to call him so he could keep me updated on their progress. In fact, he would send me the work they have done in school, some of which I still have in my possession up until today.

I used to ship books over to them as he mentioned that my children, especially Dave was very creative and read a lot. Sometimes although my children are quite grown up now, they remember those books and reminisce of those days.

On their birthdays, I was able to call them in the school and speak with them, wishing them happy birthday. Sometimes I would forget the time difference and call during lesson times; he would allow them to be called out of class so that I could speak to them. He was a very understanding man.

It got so that I could feel the weight of a package in my hands and exactly how much it was going to cost me. That was how familiar I was in the post office; I was known by the staff there.

My New Identity

I was still trying to figure out how on earth God was going to undo my mess, but very soon I realised that that was not my burden anymore. After becoming a Christian, I began to read the Bible. My spiritual mum and grandmother taught me about the fear of God and the love of God. Most importantly, they taught me about redemption. During this period I learned so much i.e. to trust God to take care of my children, and to love Him with all my heart and my soul.

I was really excited at this time in my life because as I began to experience this new identity, I realised that everything my grandmother had taught and told me she found in the Bible, and now I was beginning to find the same things.

I gained a deeper understanding of what Jesus Christ did for me on the cross. I was taught how to pray, the true meaning of prayer, which is talking to God. I learned that God speaks to us through His word, the Bible, and I found the answers to every question I had in the Bible. What amazed me the most, and still does, is that God knew me even before my mother and father knew they were going to have me. It says so in . It also says that there is no place where

I can hide from God; in my depression He was there, during the nightmares He was there, He knows my sitting down and He knows my thoughts. It goes on to say that I am "fearfully and wonderfully made" by God.

It says that all my days were written in the Bible, the Book of Life. It all started to make sense. All this time I thought I was alone but I was not. I had been in so many near-death situations, I often wondered why I did not die back then. I realised that I could not because He is the pillar that holds my life. He is the lifter of my head; He is the hope when all hope is gone. I had a chance to read a story in the Bible about Lazarus. In the story he had been pronounced dead for three days. The family believed this and his sister was telling Jesus when He showed up on the scene that if he had been there earlier her brother would not have died and now it was too late. The rest of the story goes to show that it is never too late for God.

Jesus went to the mouth of the tomb and said, "Lazarus come forth". The Bible records that Lazarus came out of his tomb and Jesus instructed the people around him to untie him. Remember that He had been dead for three days (and in those days they did not have embalming fluid to preserve the body; his body was already decaying, and the smell was really bad). In Lazarus I saw myself; I felt my life had been written off.

After reading this story it dawned on me that this was my life. I felt like Jesus was bidding me to come to Him. 'Fikelephi, come forth', he was saying. He instructed Kathy and all the helpers of my destiny to untie me, as the people in the Bible did Lazarus. All my life I had been labelled, called so many names. The words still ring: you are nothing; you will never amount to anything; you are a fool; you are a disgrace. Thank God that I now know the truth which has set me free. I pray by the mercy of God that if you do not yet know this truth, as you read my book you will get to know it. That Jesus died for you and I may have life John 10:10 reads "The devil has come to steal, kill and destroy, but Jesus has come that you and I might have life even more abundantly."

How many more lives must we lose? Because people don't know the truth, lives are lost. If only every person could know this truth that I now knew, lives would be saved just as mine was.

The Stepmother

I was still working at the hospital; it was now six months since I started. I was able to afford to speak to my children at least once a week and I was sending them all they needed.

The update from back home through Yasmin (and the children, sometimes) was that Suli had found himself another woman, Mercy, whom they addressed as their stepmother. Sadly, she was going through exactly the same abuse that I had gone through.

The abuse made her vulnerable and she found it difficult to relate to my children.

I was told that Suli used to tell her that he had a wife-to-be, me, who was coming back and she should not become comfortable in his house. Eventually, she did begin to get on with my children.

Unfortunately though; Mercy had it much worse than I did. Suli beat her up so badly one day and injured the bridge of her nose so severely that she lost her sight. She had been blind for a while when he beat her up again. This time she had to be taken to hospital. She did not survive her wounds and died in hospital.

Suli and Mercy had been married a while; she had two boys for him before she died. Only then did it dawn on me and members of my family, especially Yasmin that this could have been me, but the mercy of God said no.

Before she died she met one Holy who travelled to Africa on holiday. I would buy school clothes for my children and give them to here with the instructions to visit my children and pray for them. When she got to my house she found their step mother covered in bruises, she was in so much pain she could not even get up. She told my mentee to tell me that I was very lucky to have escaped as she knew then that she was not going to make it. My mentee prayed for her as well as the children. She too had two children for Suli.

When I had worked in the hospital for about eight or nine months, they wanted me to work for them as a permanent member of staff instead of through the agency because I was doing so well and they were very pleased with my work.

I was very reluctant to tell Walter because I was still waiting for my visa to come through and I still did not have my National Insurance number.

One day, I mentioned it to Kathy, so she prayed that my National Insurance number comes through quickly. She advised me to take a day off to visit the relevant offices for the number. I told her that I had gone there before but they did not attend to me because I did not have any form of identification – all of which I had left with the authorities in the Organisation I was to work for. All the same Kathy urged me to go explaining, that now she had prayed, I will not be going there on my own but with God. And so I did.

This time around there was something different. I believed what Kathy said. When I got to their offices, I was given a ticket with a number. I got called when it was my turn and a kind lady attended to me. The lady asked me questions and I told the truth. I told her that my papers were at the Home Office and that I had a job waiting for me once my visa comes through. She said that it was not a problem; she just needed to call the Organisation in London. After the phone call she smiled at me and wished me luck, as the Organisation's office had confirmed that I would be starting my office role shortly as they now had heard from the Home Office. She then told me that I was going to receive my National Insurance number in the post.

I called my manager, Kathy, and informed her of the good news. I was excited.

So, the big Guy upstairs does listen when you talk to Him. I was getting this now. Since the phone box incident, He had been doing the things that I or others asked concerning me.

While all this change and transformation is going on, my family on the other hand was not on the same page with me. They did not fully understand that God was turning my life around, and that everyday something was changing inside me.

They couldn't understand why now I was happy, smiling more and becoming confident in myself. It was a far cry from the desperate, moody, unsure, timid person that I was when I arrived from South Africa. Who I was becoming before their eyes was too good to be true in comparison to the woman who had a daily pity-party.

As mentioned in the previous chapter; I continued being in touch with my children; I did everything I could to make sure they knew that mummy was thinking of them and that they were loved. I thank God for sustaining them, and for sustaining me too.

A few days later, I received a call from the High Commission in London that they had received all the necessary papers from the Home Office and I could start work soon.

I gave two weeks' notice to the hospital.

CHAPTER 8

Kathy and I: By this time, I had developed a very close relationship with Kathy (mother and daughter). She taught me the Bible just the way my grandmother used to. She taught me to read the Bible and would explain things I did not understand to me. I asked her a whole lot of questions.

I was indebted to her for bringing me to a place where I wanted to know the big Guy upstairs (I had started referring to Him as God by now) just like Kathy did.

So it was with very mixed emotions that I gave in my notice. I didn't want to leave and neither did Kathy want me to as well as my colleagues.

I was going to miss the Home Group and the church I had been attending, Mr and Mrs Careen and everyone who had been a part of my growth and development as a Christian. I was really going to miss Northampton. My life had taken a new and better turn since being there.

A card and gift were given to me by the staff in the department where I worked and Kathy gave me a gift of a plaque which I kept for many years after. It said something like this:
'Your circumstances are a hindrance of seeing God's ability in your life. If you take your eyes off your circumstances and fix your eyes on God or Jesus, he will take you step by step and each step will be a miracle.'

It was signed by Morris Cerrulo. The plaque was green and the words were written in gold.

I remember the words so well because whenever I felt discouraged, I would pick it up and read it over and over again, until the words became imprinted on my heart.

When the time came for me to relocate to London to take up my position as an Information Officer within an Organisation, a part of me was very excited but the other part of me did not want to leave Northampton and all the people who were helping me. I felt like a baby, still learning how to walk; I was nowhere near ready to face society at large.

As I packed my few belongings and I prepared to leave, my sister gave me advice about living in London and warned me that it was a harsher environment compared to the small community in Northampton that I had lived in for almost a year.

Her husband who found me the job at the Organisation was very happy for me as well as other members of my family. My niece was not very happy that I was leaving. But she knew that it was for the best.

I went to the post office to let them know they will not be seeing much of me anymore and I said my goodbyes. I thanked them too because they had made a very emotional journey for me very simple.

On the day I left, my sister drove me to the train station.
I had about a two-hour journey on the train to London to look forward to.

London Welcomes Fikelephi

I rented a room, sharing a house with four other people.

This was new ground for me, I did not know these people and I was nervous.
London struck me as a very loud and boisterous environment. I decided I would keep to myself and not get too close to anyone. I felt quite exposed. I realised that North of England was a closed community and I was in safe

hands with Kathy, the Home Group members, my colleagues in the hospital and my family.

I reminded myself that I still had a responsibility towards my children and life in that regard would continue. I would still buy phone cards to call them on their birthdays and to check up on them at school.

Fikelephi's First Day

On my first day I was taken around the office by my boss. It was a huge Organisation, it had so many departments. Finally I was taken to the specific department where I would be working. My boss went through my contract with me and explained to me how things would work. I asked him a few questions.

I was to work Monday to Friday, 9am to 5pm and have an hour's break.

My boss took me through my job description and explained to me what was expected of me. He said he was responsible for getting information across to other offices and my job was to assist him and make it easier for him to get his job done.

When he left, I read through my job description again, familiarised myself with how the computer works, how to use the office diary and other pertinent matters. At 1:00pm I went outside for lunch. Although I had brought lunch from home (I had learnt from Kathy), I still went out to take a look around the part of London where my office was located.

After lunch, one or two of my new colleagues came round to my desk to find out how I was doing. At 5pm, I left for home. It was an easy and uneventful first at work in London.

My Accommodation

Sadly, there were a few issues with the house where I was staying and the other tenants moved out one by one. Eventually, I was the only one left in the house.

When I came to London for the interview I had made a new friend called Sally, who worked in the Organisation and when I found out she too had children, we made a connection. We kept in touch while I was in North of England. I had been in London for about a month when I went away one weekend to stay with Sally. When I arrived in London she invited me over to stay the weekend of her son's birthday with her. She lived on the outskirts of London.

When I came back, I discovered that the house had been broken into and the place had been turned upside down. None of my possessions were stolen but left on my bed was one of my dresses which I had not left there and on the floor were dirty, greasy large gloves. I was shaken; I thanked God for preserving me that weekend. Imagine if I had been at home this weekend, I don't know what would have happened to me.

I was very afraid. I felt someone must have been watching the house and now knew that I was the only one left there and had come to hurt me. I remembered what Kathy had told me, to call her whenever I needed to. I needed to right now. I immediately picked up the telephone and called Kathy in Northampton.

I explained to her that thieves had broken into my room and I was very scared. She suggested it would be better to go back to Sally's and also to call my landlord and ask him to make changes to the door and to the locks. I thanked her, dropped the phone and dialled my landlord.

I asked him to fix the door and change the locks or give me back my deposit. I figured I could use the money to find another place to rent. He refused. I took his lack of cooperation as a sign that I had to move out as soon as possible.

I packed a few things, added to what I had already in my luggage and called Sally telling her what had happened. She told me to come back to hers and stay until I could find another place to stay. I left immediately.

In the midst of this, that same fear that I had experienced back home when Suli abused me gripped me again. I could feel it like a cloak coming over me. I actually thought that he had hired someone to kill me or hurt me; after all, he had threatened over and over again that if I ever left him, he would track me down and he would kill me.

But the difference was that now I knew how to address this fear. Kathy had taught me to capture negative words spoken to me or about me, by counteracting them with positive words or just the complete opposite of those negative words. I had been studying the Bible so I knew a few scriptures I could use.

Thank heavens for Godly counsel and the support I was still receiving from the church. Kathy had introduced me to the branch of the church in London which I had been attending since I arrived. In fact, I was going through the baptism lessons at this time because I wanted to be baptised but it was important to me that I understand what baptism meant.

I stayed at Sally's house for almost two weeks before I found temporary. I continued to look for something more permanent accommodation.

CHAPTER 9

The Unforgettable Interview

I approached an estate agent and had a chance to view a few studio flats. None of the properties I saw appealed to me; either the asking price was higher than what I had planned to spend, or it simply wasn't the right place for me.

Just when I was about to give up, I went back to the estate agent and a lady there informed me that she was about to contact a Mr Colin Jackson. He was a landlord and preferred to meet his tenants first for an interview before he could consider them as tenants. Not only did he want to interview them, he also wanted references from their employers. Finally, I thought, I would have a proper landlord who does things properly; my prayer was that I would like one of his houses at least.

I waited patiently for Colin to arrive. Before he entered the office, I had been praying under my breath as I had been taught by Kathy. (PUT EXPRESSION LATER ON IN BOOK) I prayed that this would be it, that I would find a safe home at last.

After the introduction, Colin started to ask me questions about my job. I also had some questions for him, it turned out I was doing more of the interviewing as I had more questions than he did. But he didn't mind. In fact, he encouraged me to ask more questions if I had any.

After the initial interview, we were both happy to move on to the next level of actually viewing the available properties. When we arrived at one of his properties, I met some of his tenants whom I felt quite comfortable with. After being shown the vacant room in that property I was happy to take on the tenancy. Colin pursued my references, which were not a problem. Sadly my happiness only lasted for about two weeks, as Colin's business partner knocked on our door one day and informed us that they had decided to rent the house to a group of student doctors. He gave us all four weeks' notice to find somewhere else to live.

I could not believe my ears. I was confused and started to ask God what was going on? Somehow, in the midst of me hitting the roof, I knew that it was going to be alright, but how, I didn't know. I had stopped trying to figure out how He was going to sort me out. I was in His hands. I had given Him permission to invade my life in that telephone box.

But I had a bone to pick with Colin though. Unknown to me, Colin had told his business partner not to give me the notice but the others because he wanted to speak to me directly.

So, the very next day, he came looking for me at my office. That was good, because I needed some answers. He apologised saying that his partner should not have given me that notice as he still had another accommodation earmarked for me. I was very surprised to learn this. When I asked where the room was he told me it was in his house. No way, I thought to myself, I was not going to even consider it.

He convinced me to come and see the room. So, after work, I met up with him I went with him reluctantly. When I got there, I met his girlfriend who seemed to be a very nice person and I liked her straight away. By the time I saw my room I was happy to take it and saw it as just a continuation of my previous tenancy in his other property.

The house was homely. My concerns of living in the same house with my landlord, who happened to be a man, if you understand what I mean, were allayed.

This was close enough to the second job I found. Sally had helped me to find this job; in fact I didn't have to apply for it, the owner of the company was a friend of Sally's. Bearing in mind I had moved several times, this accommodation was just right in terms of distance and location to both of my jobs. You wonder why I had two jobs. I had to so I could continue to provide for my children back home, finish paying my mum back for the ticket and also now I was paying rent, buying food and paying for transport. I needed more money. Things had really changed for me.

Plus, this was the first time I could really sleep well through the night.

I remember I said earlier in the book that I slept peacefully through the night for the first time after I gave my life to Christ, but it was just that night because there were other nights I woke up because of a nightmare although it wasn't often. Once, Kathy had to take me away from my sister's house for a weekend for a change of environment. It did me good.

I lived in Colin's house for the next four years. During that time, I was treated as part of the family. I had the privilege of meeting all the Jackson family and I got to know them very well. Colin and I also grew close, he came to know about my challenges and about my children back home. As a matter of fact he used to take me to the markets to buy my children's clothes to send back home. I trusted my new family they trusted me and it was not long before Colin and his girlfriend started coming to church with me. He refused to be referred to as Colin, so I referred to him by his first name, Colin. My memories of my four years were so many, but I'll mention a few.

My First Christmas with the Jacksons

We went to one of Colin's sisters, Cecelia's house. The atmosphere was so pleasant and there was a lot of love and lot of laughter. I got to learn how good a cook Colin's mum was. They exchanged gifts while telling each other how much they meant to one another. I received a little gift although I had no gift for anyone. That was a little bit embarrassing. After the meal and the fun, we went back home. It was a beautiful day. It was my first Christmas I spent with a family where there was so much love.

In my village we did not exchange gifts and it was quite a large gathering, nothing close and intimate like what I had just experienced. It was really nice especially as I felt really accepted by the family. The Jackson family seemed so accommodating; they did not ask me questions.

Before I slept that night I called my children on the neighbour's phone to wish them Merry Christmas and to ask if they loved the gifts that

I had sent to them – if the clothes fitted them and the shoes too.

My Music

I used to play gospel songs by Vine Song on my portable cassette player almost every day. I played it on very low volume because I didn't want to disturb my new found family. By this time I knew all the songs on the album and they spoke to my heart in a very deep way. One day Colin requested that I turned up the volume. This took me by surprise because I didn't know he could hear the music when I played it. Later, he asked to play the cassette in his big and better stereo. It did sound better.

CHAPTER 10

Forgiveness is a Gift from God

I had added more to my walk with God. I had begun reading books written by Christians and I was now buying and listening to sermons on different titles including forgiveness on a cassette tape. The music by Vine Song also blessed me a lot.

I felt I was treading on dangerous, very delicate ground. It was in a place I didn't want to go. Whenever I thought of Suli, I felt this intense pain; it was hidden way down on the inside of me. It could not just be erased overnight. The wounds were really deep, just hearing the word 'forgiveness' was hard for me.

Where would I start? The bottom line was that I was tired; deep down I knew I was too tired to carry on like this. However, the more I allowed the peace of God to invade my space through the music, the books and the sermons and even going to church, the more I allowed my heart to confront the subject of forgiveness.

At this point, I need to bring in a few scriptures from the Bible and hopefully explain to you as best as I can as you read on.

For example, in the book of Matthew chapter 6 from verse 5 – 14 'forgive us our trespasses as we forgive those who trespass against us.' I could not get past this scripture. It meant to me that for God to forgive me, I had to forgive others. It meant I had to forgive Suli. That was a huge thing for me to do. I didn't know or think that I could do it. In fact I didn't want to forgive Suli at all. That was where I was.
Could I change? I didn't then. All I knew was that the pain was too deep for me to just accept what the Bible was saying.

Question: How am I supposed to forgive someone who was blatant about hurting me and even promised to kill me? How was I supposed to forgive a man who would beat me up in front of my own children? A man who had no honour or respect for my mother and pushed her to the ground just because she was begging him to stop hitting me? A man who would use belts, iron rods and hurtful words to hit me.   A man whom; as far as I was concerned was not human.   After all, it is humans you forgive. How?

This was a strange season in my life. God was doing a work in life.   Remember, this was a period where I was still learning about God and how He works. So forgiveness was something I battled with.

Let's put Suli aside, let's talk about me. It was very clear that not only had I carried this pain for a long while, but for myself I could not forgive myself for allowing myself to get into the situation I found myself when I was in school.

And for a long time and even up until this time, I blamed myself for allowing all these bad things to happen to me. This really was a BIG 'ask' for me.

If I was to do it, then I had to start first, with me. Followed by Suli, some of my family members; the list went on and on. I had a lot of forgiving to do it seemed. Here is another scripture.

Psalm 51 verse 10 says....(QUOTE VERSE CREATE IN ME A CLEAN HEART) Everyday would ask God to create in me a clean heart and renew the right spirit within me.

However, I knew that while I was still feeling hurt and carrying all of these baggage – hurt, shame, stigma, low self esteem, humiliation, self pity, worthlessness, cursed – all in one suitcase – that was a heavy suitcase. I had to leave it at the next airport and never reclaim it.

I desperately had to be FREE. Enough was enough. I had to let it go.

Looking back now, I can see that this was all in God's plan for me. When I prayed in the phone box about changing Walter's mind, I did not know that it was not just that answer I needed I also needed God. He set me up.

He changed Walter's mind just so I could know Him through Kathy. He knew that I will get to this season in my life where I would have to make a decision to forgive or not to forgive and He knew I would need Him to be able to do this.

But I was not ready. And even if I was, I could not do it on my own. I needed God's help. I had to allow Him to deliver me – from myself and my thoughts which seemed to hold me back.

I had to allow Him to heal me of the past hurt and the past pain that seemed to have its clutches in my heart. I had to allow Him to cleanse me because sometimes I felt physically dirty and useless. God had a lot of work to do on me, and I also had to allow Him to encourage me to do what the Bible says to do, to do the right thing by letting go of all the baggage in the suitcase. I had to leave it at the airport and never reclaim it.

To tell you the truth, it was a very, very painful process. Asking me to let go of every hurt, pain, humiliation, shame - the whole lot. Surely He must understand how painful it had been for me all these years of feeling worthlessness and accused. But He referred me to Jesus, who hung on the cross, who was bruised for MY wrongdoings. Despite all that mankind had done to His only son God forgave us anyway.

Meanwhile, I had sinned and gotten myself into a situation out of ignorance and stupidity. I needed His grace. There was no doubt in my heart that if I forgave, that would be the beginning of my freedom. By this time I had been baptised in water.

Derek Prince Comes to Town: We had a guest speaker at church called Derek Prince, author of bestselling books like "Blessing or Curse", "Rules of Engagement", just to name a few. He spent a week with us in our church, throughout that week we had services every day. This was a life changing week for me. I still believe that God sent Derek Prince for me; He dealt with deliverance from oppression, curses, past hurts and forgiveness. This was yet another Dave week for me as I asked God to show me anything that was negative inside me or in my thoughts; I wanted to know what else I was dealing with apart from needing to forgive.

I knew there was a lot of de-cluttering to be done. Things that I had allowed to settle in my life without being aware of it, I learnt I had the power through Jesus Christ to **disallow them in my life. I had a lot to renounce. I felt sick; it was like opening up wounds again. This time it was different as I knew I was drawing the line. No longer will I allow myself to be depressed over my past, enough was enough. I did not have to carry any more of the stigma.**

Completion of Deliverance Week: That's what I called it, 'Deliverance Week.' I walked through the week, it was remarkably life changing. I felt liberated and free to live my life; indeed to begin a new life. **Everything seemed to me like a new day had dawned.** I remember telling God in the telephone box that I would do whatever He made me for as long as He answered my prayer. Now it seemed like I was going to do just that with this new life I had acquired.

After a week with Derek Prince I knew I was on another level, I started encouraging and praying for people, who are oppressed, depressed or feeling like they had failed and had lost all hope.

From then on any person I met who felt like had felt, I would take time with them to help them get rid of their baggage.

I noticed that their lives would turn around for the better.

At the end of the book there are testimonies of some of the lives that have been transformed through the grace of God after they heard my life's story.

CHAPTER 11

My Three Little Angels

You are probably wondering what has been happening to my three little angels all this time. My children were doing very well at school apart from witnessing their new step-mother being beaten. After the death of the first step-mother, Mercy, Suli got yet another woman, Rosemary. This was their second step-mother. She could not have children; I do not know the full story, whether she was barren or what the issue was. Sadly, she did not see eye to eye with my children especially my daughter. I was told that because Suli did not hide the fact that he loved his children, she was probably vying for his attention; she did not like it and so took it out on my children, especially Beautiful.

At home this became more and more unbearable for them, that is, my children. By this time, I was asking God to enable me to bring them over to join me in the UK. I was missing them desperately. Some days I could not eat as I would be wondering if they had eaten or not. I know this sounds strange, over 8000 miles away, but then that is a mother's love. Whenever I looked sad, Colin would offer to get me an international phone card so I could call them and speak to them. This used to help then, and I would pray for them over the phone.

A Miracle Happens – I Visit My Children

After about eight or nine months in the Organisation, my position changed. My CEO had been receiving recommendation letters about me. As a result of this, I was promoted – the position was in the tourism department.
The CEO was a lady; and two weeks into my new role she called me into her office and informed me that part of my role is to take tour operators on educational trips to Africa. Being new to this kind of work, I knew it would be a good idea to go home and learn – this was

crucial for me as it involved southern parts of Africa, not just one country.

I was not sure where all this was going, but I knew this, there was no way I could afford a ticket to fly to any of these countries. While I stood listening to all I had to learn and do, the CEO pulled open her drawer and handed a plane ticket to me with an itinerary. As I took the documents from her, she advised that I had ten tour operators travelling with me.

Then she added, "I have given you two days in your city, as I have heard you have three children. You can spend two days with them, and then proceed with the trip." Once again I was pinching myself. Was this really happening to me? I could hardly believe my ears.

I raised my hands to hold either side of my head in surprise. I was almost in awe. In fact, you can say I was awe-struck. When I got home, I jumped up and down excitedly like a little girl. Later, I phone Kathy and told her about it. She was very happy for me.

Of course, no one knew back home that I was coming.

So, I got in contact with the children's whose Headmaster knew me so well, as stated in the previous chapters. The Headmaster told me on the phone that I brought tears to his eyes because he knew what this brief visit will mean to the children.

I was so nervous. I was not sure how Suli would react. I remember Kathy teaching me to replace the negative with the positive and as I had been reading the bible a lot more, I looked for a scripture that I could use as the positive. Let me share it with you here. There a scripture in the bible in Isaiah 54 talks about no weapon formed against me would prosper.

The whole trip was like a dream to me, I stayed in five star hotels throughout the country, I wished I was allowed to take my children with me on the tour, the whole tour.

I am still blown away by God's love and mercy towards me till this day. I thank Him every day. He told me in the plane that NOTHING WAS IMPOSSIBLE WITH HIM, He makes a way where there is no way.   Everything my grandmother taught me tallied with what the bible says; now I was seeing and still seeing His hand upon my life every day. He is amazing to me.

My spiritual mum, Kathy, that is who she became to me, told me that God promised that he was going to take my life step by step, that each step was going to be a miracle. I remember she gave me a gift of a plaque where those words were written and I used to read them over and over again. She was right. The words were true.

Whereas before I used to curse the day I was born. Now **I thank him for the day I was born, for the gift of life.**

CHAPTER 12

Back to the Jackson Household

After two years of working in the Organisation, I was made redundant along with a few of my colleagues. This was a big blow as my Visa was attached to my position there. I prayed, asking God for direction. He knew I had no plan B, I depended entirely on God Him.

First, one of the Tour Operators decided to take me on. When they realised this meant they had to apply for my Work Permit too, they were reluctant. I was very concerned now for Colin who had been so kind to me. Now I was out of work, I could not afford to pay the rent anymore – if I didn't get another job very soon.

During this time, Linda came to see me. She knew I had been made redundant and brought me news that she had a job waiting for me outside London as well as accommodation.

When I informed Colin of this, he asked me why I wanted to move out. I told him I could not afford to pay the rent anymore. The next thing he said surprised me. He said, "Not to worry; when you get another job resume making the payments."

I kept on looking for work for five or six months, especially as I was settled in London, albeit, I was grateful for the offer.

While I was out of work, I could not feed myself as I used to. So, Colin would include me in all the meals that were cooked in the house. I was really grateful for his selfless attitude. I didn't know anyone could be so kind.

28 Days Remaining On My Visa

When I had 28 days left on my visa, I began praying furiously. I told God if he wanted me to go back home to where my children are, I was happy to. After all, I was now a better person than I was when I first of all came to the UK and that was all because of God. Little did I know that he was yet to **restore my life.**

Every Sunday, I would go to church and attend every single service – the 9am, 11am, 2pm and the evening service at 7.30pm. But this day, I did not go to church because I decided I might as well begin to prepare to return to my home country. I did not want to be in the UK illegally so, I went to the market instead to buy two large suitcases and brought them home ready to pack begin packing my belongings because by this time, I had only ten days left.

When I came back from the market, Colin was shocked when he learnt that I was planning to travel back to Africa. He did not realise that this would be the consequence of not finding a job. He said we had to talk. He sat me down and managed to talk some sense into me.

He said he didn't think that I had explored all my options. He asked me how I knew that Suli would not try to hurt me again when I returned. He suggested that there were other things that I could try that there must be another way.

This was a prayer answered for me. I had asked God to speak to me or send me a sign if I should go or not.

Colin and I had a heart to heart chat and by the time we finished I knew that my answer was there, i.e. God had made a way already, it was only a matter of time before I would find the way.

He Makes a Way Where There Is No Way

Colin called his business partner the following morning, the same one who had given me notice in the other house. It turned out he had

a position for a PA – Personal Assistant and he
was willing to make the application to the Home
Office on my behalf.   His offices were in
London, I went for an interview and I got the
position.

I was grateful that I was still in the country
legally after six months of being out of
employment.   I worked with Colin's partner as
his PA for almost two years.

My being out of work caused my relationship
with Colin to grow.   We would do things
together around the house.   We got quite close.
And I became close to his girlfriend too and not
just her but to the other Jacksons.   It was such
a lovely relationship we had among ourselves.

For personal reasons, Colin had to travel
abroad for a while.   In his absence I had to
move out to find somewhere else to live because
he wanted to sell the property.   During this

period things were not so great for me, first my job as PA came to an end right about the same time that I had to move house. Suddenly I had no home and no job.

Homeless and Jobless

I went to the homeless offices, who at first did not want to know about my case as they felt my status in the country was not permanent. I was so discouraged as a result; I insisted that they needed to hear me out as I had nowhere to go. After a long wait towards the end of the day at 17:05 they decided to put me in a hostel for the weekend.

I went to the hostel and I stayed there for the weekend. I spent it with God praying and reading the bible. This time I trusted him entirely, my life was entirely in his hands, according to his promises his thoughts towards me are good, not evil.

While there, I found out that I couldn't go out anywhere because I would lose the room. It was common knowledge that if I left even to visit someone, the authorities would think that I had somewhere to stay. So I stayed put for the whole weekend.

On Monday I was one of the first in the queue. When my name was called, I was taken aback. The staff were suddenly very eager to attend to me. I did not understand why.

I later learnt that while I had busy praying and talking to God throughout the weekend, some of my church leaders had been looking for me because I had not shown up for my duties at church as was my habit to do. They knew something was wrong because I had never missed a day before. They started searching for me and only stopped when they got information through the homeless offices.

When they mentioned my name to the homeless officers, they confirmed that I was in one of their hostels. The officers began asking for more information about me. My church leaders substantiated the information I had already given them which led to their giving me a studio flat. Three months later, one qualified for a 1-bedroom flat which was allocated to me.

Colin Is Back In The Country:

I was overjoyed when I heard Colin was back in the country.
I am sure you are wondering why.
Well, he was one person I could speak to without feeling any inhibitions at all. To me, he had become a good and trusted friend.

He was sad to learn about my happenings; at the same time he was pleased that I had got my own flat. We continued going to church together with the family and sometimes I would have lunch at the Jackson's and vice versa.

You see, I did not live far from them and this was quite convenient especially when I did not feel like cooking.

A few months after Colin returned, he told me that he and his girlfriend were no longer together. She had also told me the same thing earlier. She told me she had made the decision based on the fact that she did not believe that Colin was for her because she had become a Christian and had been praying about it. She believed that if she stayed with him, she would delay her own Mr Right and vice versa. It was a very amicable separation.

Meanwhile, I continued being very active in church, I was grateful for every opportunity, I realised then and still do that it's a privilege to serve God. I was beginning to feel much better about myself. My children were doing well at school and I missed them desperately.

I was also beginning to believe that maybe there was a slight chance that I would one day be happy, most importantly it was dawning on me that every pain I had gone through was for my good and maybe someday, I would be able to help others going through similar difficult times and encourage the hurting and discouraged. I felt my purpose was unveiling right in front of me.

Colin & Fike Yvone
ChakaChaka & Husband

CHAPTER 13

Time Is A Healer They Say...Or Is It?

There were a few eligible bachelors who were very interested in dating me. One of them was Colin's business associate who had asked me out a few times, but I had turned him down. I had made up my mind that I would not make another big mistake – and knew God heard me.

One of these bachelors had been pursuing me for over a year. I thought to myself, it was probably time to give things a chance but first, I had to speak to my friend, Colin. Aside from the fact that I trusted Colin, he knew this particular bachelor and I valued his opinion and so wanted to know his thoughts.

His response was not positive; he believed that I was very special and delicate, that I needed someone who would understand where I was coming from and someone who would accept the children too. He concluded by saying it was up to me what I wanted to do.

Nevertheless, I called this person and invited him to dinner in my flat. I was nervous but, this time around I had a sense that I wasn't alone like I was with Suli. Dinner was wonderful, and I was completely aware of all that was going on around me. There was no ignorance at all. During dinner the gentlemen made a point of reminding me of his intention to marry me if I would have him. He added that there was something he needed to tell me.

Oh! Oh! Here We Go Again

He dropped the bombshell!
He told me something that rattled my secure but still fragile mind. He informed me that although he had been pursuing me and is still interested in me, he had had a one night stand and the girl had fallen pregnant, but I was not to worry about this. He had already told the girl that he intends to marry me but he would take care of the baby.

I suddenly lost my appetite. I had known this guy for about two years. I asked him why he had not told me this before. This was a loud and clear sign that I should run a mile away from this man. I thanked him for dinner and asked him to leave. I thought he was different but he was just another man. Here I was, thinking that I knew this person even after two years. It takes a much longer time to get to know a person, any person.

I felt like a fool once again, I hated myself for this, all the negative thoughts started invading my mind again, for a moment I forgot what my spiritual mum, Kathy had taught me, how to counteract negative thoughts with positive words from the Bible.

Colin was right, this man was not the right person for me; he was right that I was very delicate; I was not ready for this. He could have been anyone.

But let me address another aspect of this incident.

It was not wise, now with hindsight, that I should have invited him to my flat for dinner. I actually cooked. Even though I had known him for a while, it was not sensible. Although I was not in my flat on my own with him, my flatmate was home, I did not know the man enough to have had him over. It was not in good taste.

A message to you young women who aren't yet married or are engaged: get to know, really know the man you are interested in or who is interested in you. One way of doing this is to meet in public places and to be accountable.

I had accommodated Holly, a young lady who had travelled down to stay with her family but who let her down, subsequently she had no place to stay. I knew what this felt like and so was happy to give her a place to rest her head, eat and keep warm.

She attended church with me and had enrolled in our Bible College. She became like a sister to me and we prayed together a lot. Holly also got to know about my three little angels back home.

The day after dinner with my date, I had a migraine attack. These migraines started as a result of the beatings or whenever I was worried or stressed. This was still an on-going prayer request to God, prayer for complete healing even from migraines. I was disappointed with myself. Then Colin called on the phone. I told Holly to tell him I could not come to the phone as I had a bad migraine.

Remember I had lived with him for four years, so during this time I would speak to him with or without migraine. I had forgotten that he knew me that well. His response was, "I know something is wrong, Fikelephi would speak to me whether she has a migraine or not. In that case tell her I'm coming over."When Holly relayed this message to me, I decided that I would rather I speak to him on the telephone than for him to come to my flat and see how an embarrassed Fikelephi looks even though he knows what that look like.

When I took the phone, he straight away said, "It's him is it not?" I was silent knowing what he was about to say i.e. "I told you so, did I not?"

I was so ashamed of myself; I should have listened to him.

Over the next months that followed Colin encouraged me. He said I should thank God that nothing happened, it was a blessing in disguise, and I should not worry myself.

I got back on track, but this time, there was no looking back. My aim was to serve God, find out what I was created to do and focus on God and my children. I must say here I knew that part of my calling was to help other people; still it was not crystal clear. The fact that Holly was living with me was evidence of this 'help' I was to offer others because I helped her time and again.

Surprise! Surprise!.

One day, Colin called me and told me he had something to talk to me about. I did not know what was on his mind.

Later that day, we met up to talk. I was quite curious, it sounded serious.

He told me that he believed that God had shut all doors for a reason. I did not understand this; what doors was he talking about? He reminded me that his ex-girlfriend left him because she believed he was not the one for her. I had attempted starting a relationship with the bachelor. Again, God shut that door because he was not the one for me.

I was becoming increasingly confused and baffled all at the same time. I was trying to understand where this conversation was going. He asked me how I felt about the bachelor. I told him I was thankful that nothing happened that it was really a blessing in disguise. We went down 'imagination lane' when we wondered what havoc would have been created if I had entered into a relationship with him. After my past...oh, that would have been disastrous.

Then, surprise! And I was really surprised! We were in a café; we just needed a quiet place to talk. Colin spoke scented words...or so I thought – after the fact.

He said, "Fikelephi, I love you and I want to be with you forever. I want to marry you." I could not believe what I was hearing. I had known him for over four years. What was he saying? I asked him to break it down for me and he did, he spelt it out.

He said, if he had made a move towards me earlier, I would not have accepted; what with all the things happening to me and around me. I had to agree with him there.

But this was too much for me. Had Colin just proposed to me or was I dreaming? I asked to end the conversation because I had to go back to my flat to pray and think about what he had just said. I told him to go back to his house.

The following day I spoke to my prayer partner, Sally, who said, "Oh, he has finally told you, has he?" She told me she could see it all the time. I thought she had lost her mind.
I told my mum, who also followed in Sally's footsteps; and the list went on. There were a few other people I spoke to who knew both Colin and I.

Then I thought I needed my mentor's input and some Godly counsel. I called her, she was one of the elders in my church and she said the same as everyone else. She told that my case was different and delicate and God knew it would take a special person to handle me with care. She advised me to seek God in prayer on the matter He would direct me accordingly.

So, I took time out to seek God concerning whether I should accept Colin's proposal to marry him; it took me several weeks.

While I was praying, I avoided calling him or even meeting up with. It was an awkward situation.

After a while it was clear to me that he was the one.

Shortly after my mind was made up, Colin rang and I told him I was ready to talk. He asked me if it was good news or bad news. I answered by saying, it depends on how he takes it.

He came over immediately with a bottle of champagne. He said to Holly that he wanted to witness something because he had something to say.

He went into the kitchen for three glasses.

Then he went on bended knees before me and said, "Fikelephi (he called all of my three names), will you marry me?"

I answered, "Yes, I will marry you."

He proceeded then to pour champagne into each of the glasses. We took sips and that was the beginning of my journey to becoming Mrs Colin Jackson.

I was officially in love with Mr Colin Jackson.

Right at that moment, I thought to myself, God must really, really love me.

I admired and had great respect for Colin and highly valued his advice. He was, to me, and still is, a disciplined and astute man; he was quite a catch.

The news was well received by both families; they were all excited for us.

Our First Outing

Colin, of course wanted to take me out on a date, our very first date but I already had this invitation from my sister's children, my niece and nephew.

They are both musicians and were playing in a very prestigious venue in the town where they lived and had invited me to come and watch them. I suggested to Colin that we could go down together and watch them. He agreed.

Our first date was a drive down to go and watch them play after which we had dinner.

The drive down was beautiful; it took about one and a half hours – just the two of us. And we drove back the same day. It was one and a half hours long coming back too. Three long hours spent with Colin on my own and in love with him for the first time – that was different. This was a new season for me. I had not been here before. I was excited and at peace. I was not sure how everything was going to turn out.

We went on so many other dates after this one and courted for a year before we finally got married.

Different Worlds Come Together

To my surprise, God had it all in hand. Colin told me that one thing he was looking forward to was going through the process of negotiations, paying the dowry (Lobola) the whole lot. He said he was going to do so with much pride, as he planned to marry me properly.

Thankfully my eldest brother was still alive. After being such a disappointment him with Suli, now he was to become a father in-law in the true sense of the word. Colin was really eager to learn more about my culture. He went with a notebook and took notes of the step by step process of what needed to be done before the traditional wedding.

He did all he had to do and did it very well. It would take a long time to describe every step that he took, but believe me; he paid the dowry (Lobola). We did the traditional wedding shortly after. This was very important to my family. You can imagine how I felt. Finally, I was doing things right as they should be done.

We planned the white wedding over the next several months. Colin and I worked so well together. I recall thinking that I must be dreaming. Was I really going to walk down the aisle with this wonderful man, after giving birth to three children? Yes, I was. This had seemed like an impossible dream. I had believed in a lie for so long. I had believed that I was not loveable, that Suli was right and the voodoo man had confirmed it too. Yet here I was planning my own wedding.

Every Girl Has A Dream Dress

I remember when I went to Oxford Street in search of my perfect dress. I went with Sally and Holly. I had the style of my dress in my head a long train with bows at the back. When I got to Oxford Street I went straight to Berketex; a friend of mine who had recently got married recommended the store to me. It turned out they had a 'special bride's day' when all the dresses were being sold at half price.

I had prayed that morning that God would take me to where my dress was.

As I looked through, there it was everything I had imagined. I asked the shop assistant if I could try it. She took me to the changing room. I am not exaggerating this was the most beautiful dress I had ever seen. The shop assistant said to me, "this dress was made for you." She could not stop telling me how

beautiful I looked. She was right; once again God had exceeded my expectations.

I paid a little deposit and came back for it later with the rest of the payment.

Later, Colin and I called my children to tell them the good news that mummy was getting married; this was good news because he had every intention of helping to bring them over when the time was right.

The Big Day Arrives

Before the big day, my fiancé and I had been going through Marriage Preparation classes in our church for several months. This was great because I learnt so much, one of the key things I learnt was that **marriage is a covenant; it's a gift from God. My husband is a gift from God to me.**

Food is usually a big part of the wedding, as you know. The owner of the venue that we wanted to use also provided the catering. When we initially met with them they asked us for our menu, we submitted this to them. Our special request was to cater for three types of meals West Indian, African and British dishes.

The menu was perfect for us, but they turned around and said they could not do it. They showed us their own set menu which is what they could offer. We felt our African and West

Indian guests would not really enjoy it but what could I do.

We agreed to their set menu however, they took our menu with them. I did wonder then why since they had said they could not do it. Meanwhile, we went around apologising to our invited guests, before the wedding day that we would not be able to cater for everyone's taste.

But, when we arrived at the venue on our wedding day, they had a surprise for us; **everything we had requested (our dream Menu) was on the serving table. Our guests could not believe it. I was so surprised. It really was a nice touch indeed.**

I had six bridesmaids and my husband had six groomsmen. They were all our nephews and nieces as well as Sally and Holly. We wanted to inspire the next generation by showing them that marriage is a possibility and is a good thing.   Those days, and it has been about 20 years since we have been married, the younger generation did not believe in the sanctity of marriage anymore.   There was a lot of 'living together' without being married even then and still now.   We had family members suggesting that it would be okay for Colin and I to live together after all, we had lived together before anyway.   They felt there was no reason for us to get married.

We were Christians, there are principles that we live by and these principles we chose to adhere to, one being to get married before we can live together because that is right in God's eyes.   This was very important to us.

Without a shadow of doubt there was something special about our wedding.   There was so much peace, fun and love.   One could see **hope** in the eyes of our guests; there were a lot of tears of joy too.   20 years later, I still see the hand of God. Our wedding picture hangs in our living room, each time we look at it we marvel and thank God.

We prayed that as a result of our wedding, marriages will spring forth and that God would restore any marriage that was troubled. We prayed that God would give people hope in every situation.

My mother who attended the wedding, sang for us; this brought tears of joy to my eyes. After letting her down, this day she was a proud mother of the bride.

On the morning of my wedding day, however I cried because my children could not be there and I wished that my father would have been the one to give me away and not my brother-in-law. Aside from this, that day was the best day of my life.

Colin & Fike with the
Children in Africa

CHAPTER 14

It's Not Over Yet

Though my day was the best, the picture was still incomplete without my children. I knew that this would be yet another hurdle.

Holly got married shortly after we did. While she was with me, she saw the agony and pain I was going through, how much I missed my children, the phone calls, the birthdays, you name it. We had been apart for eight years by this time – and that was a very long time. They had grown.

What I did not know was that God had sent Holly to me. I will tell you what I mean.

When she went back to Africa for her wedding, we helped as much as we could financially, towards the trip. After her big day her husband told her he had a surprise for her. He took her to their new home; you will never believe that it was round the corner from where my children lived.

They Were Not Forgotten

Her husband told her when he was looking for their house that he didn't think it was a coincidence that he found a house in the same area where my children live and he believed that it was probably a plan for them to help me get my children over to the UK.

Despite the abuse, Suli loved his children; but with hindsight now, I see that it was a possessive kind of love; love in itself is not possessive. More than anything he had been adamant that no one will ever take his children away from him. I knew it would be a miracle to get them over to the UK.

By the time Holly went back to get married, he was living with their second stepmother, Rosemary, who sadly could not have any children, and resented my children, especially my daughter, Beautiful. She took out her frustrations of being abused by Suli on them. My children were suffering in the hands of this woman.

Thank God for Holly, my God-given sister who became my children's 'angel.' She alongside Yasmin, kept me informed on what they needed among other things. All together, the six of us – Colin and I, Yasmin and Holly along with their husbands with God's help started the journey to getting the children out of Africa. First things first we had to get passports for them. We prayed and fasted.

One day, I felt it was time after much prayer and summoning up the courage; I called Suli and asked if I could have the children over for holiday. He told me he would think about it.

I called him again after a few days.   He
reluctantly agreed but with the proviso that I
promise to bring them back.   I said I would.
That was all good and proper.   But none of
them had passports.   I had to get those first.

Once Suli agreed to allow the children over for
holiday, I told him I had authorised Holly,
whom he had met by then, to help with the
running around of applying for their passports.
I explained to him that because I knew he
worked he may not have the time to do this.   I
pleaded with him that he should please
cooperate with Holly and provide any
documents that she might need to pursue this.

He agreed to do so.
Yasmin worked with Holly but more in the
background.

I started thinking God is so cool.   Whenever I
prayed He answered.   I could now start to

believe that one day I would see my children with my eyes. Before, it seemed to be a complete impossibility.

It took a while for their passports to come through. This was because it depended on what mood he would be in whenever Holly visits to request some other documents.

Holly was very wise. If he was in bad mood, we had agreed that Holly would not broach the subject.

If he was stalling, she would be nice and wisely cajole him for the information she required.

Holly was very patient.

Meanwhile, whatever mood Suli was in, we carried on praying that God would soften his heart.

One day, after about five or six months, I received a phone call from Holly. She asked me if I was sitting down, I told her I was. She then broke the news that all the three passports

were ready. We agreed with both our husbands
that she could not give these to their father
because once he has them in his possession; he
was bound to change his mind.
We thanked God for answered prayer.

Now, the next stage was to get the funds to fly
them over.

The Children Fly to the UK

Because we had spent a lot of money trying to
get the passports as well as run our home here
in the UK plus I was now on maternity leave,
we were not as financially buoyant as we
needed to be

How could this be happening at such a crucial
time?
Miraculously God provided – again. I received a
phone call from a friend in the USA who told
me he had been praying for me and God told
him to bless me. He wanted to sponsor my

daughter's trip to the UK. I was moved by this because I had not asked for anything from him or from anyone. I knew it had to be God.

My daughter was the first one to arrive in the UK, the day of her arrival; we took all our passports and other documents that would identify us. When I was preparing for Beautiful arrival, I had heard all sorts of stories of parents spending hours and hours in the airport before they could see their children and sometimes they were refused. So, I planned to go well prepared.

But to our surprise, when we got to the airport, I was asked to come to the phone to speak to an immigration officer. He asked me three or four questions and he said to me, "Mrs Jackson, I believe you are Beautiful mother; I do not need to see you. Your daughter is beautiful enjoy her; she is coming down to meet you now." What a moment this was for me.

Tears of joy were rolling from my eyes down my cheeks as I saw her coming down. I went down on my knees and embraced her.

We took Beautiful home and introduced her to her siblings. Please note, that in order to respect their privacy, my four children born in the UK have been mentioned in this book before Betiful arrived.

The battle was half won. I still had to get my boys over but I had no clue how I was going to achieve this financially.   My husband, our prayer partners and I had believed God for this to happen. And yes, miraculously God made a way for the boys; they arrived a few months after Beautiful.

Again my husband and I took all our documents. When we arrived at the airport, Dave and Shepherd were standing with a lady and had a sash across their chest with the word 'minor.'

The lady couldn't stop telling me how adorable my boys were.

I was flooded with tears of joy.

This was too good to be true.

It was as if I was dreaming.

Once again we thanked God for making a way.

All Together Now

Finally the family was reunited; we had all our seven children under the same roof for the first time. Please do not think I had lost my mind because at night time I would go around and check if they are all okay in bed and give them a kiss each on their cheek.

You must be wondering how big our house is. While we were still in the one bedroom flat, after the wedding we prayed for a bigger house in preparation for our children's coming. And once again God answered. We were given a four bedroom maisonette. This did not just happen, the housing officers did not want to hear about my case as they insisted there were no big properties available.

One day, however, God brought a Councillor to my area and he got to know about my case. He said he would visit my flat on a Saturday. I did not know that he would come at 7:30am whilst the children and Holly were still asleep.

I had a knock on the door and it turned out it to be the Councillor. We could not open the door fully for him to come in because at night we had to blow up an air bed which Holly slept in at night while one of the other children used the couch and other such arrangements we had to make every single night. My husband and myself shared our bedroom with the little ones.

Holly had offered to come back to the UK to look after Dillon whom I had given birth to after Beautiful had arrived.

She and her husband had discussed her coming over to help me out by taking care of

Dillon while I went to work. We needed more income in order to take care of our large family.

So for a year, Holly lived with us and served us in the capacity of childminder. She was of course paid for her services.

After being such an awesome help to us in getting the children to the UK, I could not have asked for a more faithful, industrious and dependent sister.

When we were able to let him in, he was shocked at what he saw and assured me that he would personally report back his findings to the higher authorities. By Monday, I got a call from the senior manager of the Housing Office requesting me to come to their offices urgently.

On my arrival I was offered a drink. These were the same people who said I did not have a case. I did not understand, it brought back memories of the when I had to

stay in the hostel and then suddenly they
became nice to me. I knew then that God
had stepped in like He did then.
On this day they informed me that they had
three four bedroom properties for me to
view. None of these were suitable, in fact I
couldn't consider one of the properties at
all because of the area it was located.

I prayed and asked God not to put my
children in any danger because they had
suffered enough. I went back to the office
to let them know that I could not consider
any of the properties; they asked me to view
a fourth property. It was perfect. It was a
beautiful four bedroom maisonette.

Finally, the all the children, Colin and I were
now safe under the same roof in a house big
enough for all of us. We had a lot of things to
do, people to see, schools to visit, meetings to
attend, doctors' surgeries to register in, and a

lot of mouths to feed. It was such an exciting time in my house hold.

The Different Happenings In My Household

I had prayed and asked God that when my children come to join me; that God was going to minister to each one of them; that God loved them and that he had a plan and a purpose for their lives. We introduced our children to our local church. God answered our prayer as all the six of them gave their lives to Christ during their Sunday school teaching.

From then on; we began to have family devotions in our house. In view of our huge responsibility as parents to seven children, God miraculously provided for us. We did not lack. This is what God did. He sent a family, some friends of ours, who had become our prayer partners, approached me out of blues, and told me that God told them to help my family.

Every month this family will pick up two of my elder children and go to the supermarket with a shopping list. They would fill the cupboards with food. This continued for almost 12 months. If ever I had seen a miracle, this was it. No matter how strongly I objected to what they did, they refused to stop informing me that I was not there when God instructed them to provide for my family until my husband and I were able to by ourselves.

Meanwhile, the children were adjusting to their new environment; as their parents, we supported them all the way through. Also between themselves as siblings this was new ground for them. The bigger ones were becoming teenagers, this was not only a change of life, the whole season had changed for them well what a time for them. I devoted myself as a mother to getting to know my children; by spending time with them, talking to them about the past. I encouraged them to talk about what they had been through; not to bottle it all up inside.   As they disclosed their happenings; there were a lot of tears shared.   There were times we talked and none of us wanted to go to bed.

Our First Christmas

Our first Christmas as a family was memorable for all of us.   My husband and I ensured that the children took part in the planning and preparations.   After a long discussion we all agreed we wanted a big Christmas tree and lots of beautiful decorations.   The children in decorated the tree and Colin and I helped.

My husband and myself gave each child some pocket money to buy presents for one another. I gave each child a bag with their name on it to put their presents in.   We agreed on the schedule of the day.   It went like this:

1. Morning my husband and the boys were to cook/prepare brunch for the family in the morning and serve the family.

2. After brunch they would do the washing up.

3. Pray and thank God for reuniting us again as a family. Thank him for the presents.

4. Opening of presents; starting with the youngest. Each gift would be opened and read from where it came from. You can imagine this process would take a few good hours. The excitement and the life; the sparkle in the children's eyes; was amazing.

5. The girls and I then would cook and serve dinner and dessert and wash up after.

6. Movie time; after all the feasting then follows movie time. What a wonderfu time we had.

From then on this became our pattern or Christmas day for the following years until this day.   By this time one of the patterns we adapted was holding family meeting and one to ones with each child.   We also had a rota for chores and cooking; this gave my husband and I a chance to teach our children how to cook; clean and other life skills.

One of the items we included during our first Christmas was to go through our family album. **Flash back:** During **the ten years** whilst the children were still in Africa; God made it possible for us to visit them after we got married; this trip coincided with our chief bridesmaid's wedding; she was now getting married.   As you can imagine this was the first time that all our children met.   It was like a dream as they all just clicked liked they had known each other for years.   For me; I had mixed feeling as I knew that in a week's time I would bid them goodbye; not knowing when next I would see them.   We took a lot of pictures and made an album ***see a few of**

them below.   So in conclusion our first Christmas together will always be the best ever.

Suli tried to sabotage the visit. I had told him that I was coming over with my husband. I knew my rights in terms of fearing him because this time I knew that my husband was with me and would protect me. The children were older now and so when Suli went to pick them, they refused to go with him saying they knew mummy was coming for them. It was quite nerve racking just to visit the house. But we ended up seeing the children like we had planned. I do not want to go too much into this time, but we have pictures till today of that trip.

Leaving them was the hardest thing that I had ever done.   Beautiful and Angel were inseparable during this trip. We took them to the zoo and night time I read bed time stories to them. We spent only ten days with them.

This was an exciting time for me as a mother; at the same time very challenging as I began to learn how each child was very different from the other.   For example my first son is a relational person; he writes and had been writing since his childhood; he also enjoyed spending time with me. Whereas one of my other sons was very reserved and sensitive, I had to think through what I wanted to communicate with him before I did. While my first daughter was very girly; girly and my younger daughter a bit of a tom-boy

CHAPTER 15

Maternity Leave Over, Back to Job Hunting

My husband helped me as always; to revamp my CV. After praying about the job; I hit the streets of London; I went to an agency in Holborn who told me a company in London was hiring staff. I had to go for an interview my husband drove me. The panel finished with me they told me I would hear from them in two week's time. I left to join my husband who had been patiently waiting for me outside the Tower of London.

As we drove home; my phone rang and it was the one of the ladies who interviewed me. She started by apologising that they know that they told there to get back to me in two week's time. But they realised there was no need to wait that long and that the job was mine; would I consider to start the following Monday.

When we got home broke the news to our children; they were overjoyed as they had prayed for me to get the job. My new position came with its own challenges; as the hours were not favourable to the family routines; in the sense that I had to work most weekends especially Sundays. This meant that I would miss going to church and not function in my capacity; in my different roles in church.

One interesting thing about my new position was that we had long breaks; i.e. first tea break in the morning for 20 minutes; second lunch time midday for one hour; third break late in the afternoon around 3:00pm. I prayed that God will teach me to use my time wisely. I started doing prayer walk over the Tower Bridge; back to London Bridge and back to the Tower of London. This took place every day for 40 minutes. This exercise served two purposes of which the first one was to spend time with God in prayer and the second one was to lose weight after having a baby i.e. my last son. I worked at the Tower of London for two years.

As I was approaching the third year I began to feel very restless; asking God if I was not praying right; where was I going wrong? I had been asking for a change of position for a while. A 9:00am to 5:00pm position where I would be able to go to church and also spend time with my family. Then I decided to combine my prayer with fasting; I pleaded with God, I was exhausted.

The following week of my fasting; prayer walk; and worship. I was ready to walk over the Tower Bridge, I sensed in my spirit that I needed to walk a different way. Towards the Docks where the Thistle Tower was; this was during my first tea break. I could not believe that I had worked next door for two years plus; and knew nothing about this beautiful place.

I decided to pop into the big Thistle Tower hotel to use the ladies room; even the ladies room was spectacular. I met a maid inside the toilet who was cleaning.   I started a conversation with her. Asked her how long she had worked for the company; it turned out she had worked there for a couple of years. Asked her if they had any office positions going; she then directed me to the personnel department which was within the hotel.

I decided to go straight there knowing I had been praying for a change; remembering my experience with God how he had made a way for me in the past; where there seemed to be no way. When I got there, I met with the manager there. She straight away acknowledged that I worked next door; as I was still wearing the uniform from the Tower of London. She asked me a few questions; i.e. what type of position was I looking for and briefly my experience in my past positions etc.   The manager then started telling how strange it was that they had the position which has been advertised internally for the past couple of months; the position as for Business Secretary and it was a 9:00am to 5:00pm position.   She asked if I could come back to meet the manager for this department and his name was Mark.

This was not a problem to me as I still had two more breaks to take before the end of the day; my lunch time being the next one. I went back to work; my next break could not come any sooner; I was watching the clock and looking forward to meeting Mark.

As soon as it was lunch time I went straight to the hotel; where Mark was waiting for me together with the Personnel Manager I had met earlier.   The interview lasted for 30 minutes; they both told me I would hear from the soon.

I still had a few minutes to pray before I went back to work; my first prayer was thanking God for the interview; I told him that I trusted him entirely and I believed he heard my prayer. When I got back to work I had butterflies in my belly; I sensed something was about to happen.

A Phone Call Changes My Life

I was minding my business; still praying underneath my breath when the phone rang. It was the Thistle Tower hotel; the personnel manager asking my manager for my reference. My manager got off the phone; her face looked shocked, she asked me directly, "Fikelephi are you leaving us? That was the Thistle Tower hotel manager asking for your reference. They also asked if you could pop back on tea break to sign your contract." My heart jumped; I responded by telling her that I had only just had my interview during my lunch break.

The rest is history; I worked for The Thistle hotels for six – seven years. During those years; I met the most prominent people and made some good friends. Also during my service there; I received so many awards for being best employees. Good reports from both Mystery shoppers and guests. Part of my job as a Business Secretary was to look after VIPs in the hotel (Cooperate guests mostly from banking industries as our location was near the City).

The rewards were so much. As staff we got staff discounts; this gave me an opportunity to go on family holidays with my family; during the years at the Tower we were able to tour the UK; just to name a few Thistle in Brighton; Thistle in Poole; Alton Towers etc. This was big deal for my children and I. Year in year out they will search through the booklet which had the list of hotels my company owned throughout the country; we booked in advance for the children were on their school holidays. The incentives really helped as would not have been able to afford to go abroad on family holidays. We were all grateful that we could have a holiday; I knew that the time would come when we would all go abroad on holidays.

I used to have funny conversations with God; I knew that the season I was in was to continue bonding and getting to know my children. Also during the time I was working very closely with Total Woman Ministries; the Leader took me under her wing and my role was to help look after the Guest Speakers when they fly over for the Conferences we used to organise for women.

This gave me an opportunity of meeting other survivors; in some cases victims. I was able to encourage them having been there before. One time remember we had a big Conference forth coming; in our advertisement we encouraged women to book accommodation in advance as these were in the summer months (peak season). One of the delegates called me from Birmingham. She told me it was seven of them coming for the conference they needed affordable accommodation in London. I sent her all the good value for money hotels and B & B. As things turned out; for whatever reasons the women were not able to book in advance. They still made it to the conference; with the intention of meeting myself; they hoped I would assist them in finding accommodation for the night. I left the venue where the conference was to get back to the hotel to ensure dinner was okay for our guest speakers (Jackie McCullough; Paula White and Sharon Stone).

Some of the memorable times in my position were meeting prominent figures like Paula White from Tampa Florida; she is the one who inspired me to write a book when she had briefly my testimony. She told me that every pain I had been was not in vain. As God would use this to restore and help other people; this was my calling. She briefly told me about her own story and signed her book for.

I had an opportunity to meet Mike Murdock who also signed his books for me; who could I forget meeting legends like Donnie McClurkin & Alvin Slaughter. There is a yearly conference that takes place every year and it is called The Gathering of Champions. All the Guest speakers coming from abroad would stay in our hotel and I had a privilege of meeting them. In most cases they used to pray for me.

To everything there is a season; a time for things to begin and for things to end. I strongly felt that my time at the Thistle Tower was coming to an end; once again I began to feel restless. I was grateful for the opportunity now was time to move up. During my seven years a the Thistle Tower Thistle hotel I got head hunted twice by two reputable Banks; sadly turned both of them down as I did not think I was Banking material.

Another Day Dawns

Once again my husband and I worked on updating my CV. We called a meeting with the children; informed them that their mother on a mission to find a position that would hopefully lead to fulfilling career. My CV was sent to as many recruitment agencies as possible. Interviews started coming through; since I worked full time; the logical thing to do was to take a day off the just interviews.

On that particular day I had three interviews in Central London. I remember praying that morning; I remember how God had been faithful; since he had done before that he would do it again. I read my bible and that morning I read that the steps of the righteous are ordered by the Lord. I asked him to order my footsteps to my next office as I believed it was time.

My first interview went well I thought; so did the second one. After this one I needed time out with God; I had to get a cup of tea and some lunch. When I got to the restaurant it turned out I did not have enough coins. I asked for directions for the nearest cash machine; these directions lead me to Hanover Square at the back of Oxford Street. Yes there was more than one machine; in fact there were all the big four Banks in front of me; I had to choose which Cash Machine I was to use. Yes Halifax it had to be as it was next to Prêt a Mange; the plan was that I would get the money; then go next door and have lunch and my tea before my next interview. I took £10.00 out of the machine; I paused for a minute before proceeding to Prêt a Manger.

As I did this the doors swung wide open something happened in my spirit; I could hear the spirit of God in me telling go in there and ask for a position. What? I was responding back reminding God this was a Bank and I did not think it was my thing at all. This time I knew the voice of God clearly; he reminded me that in the morning I had asked him (given him permission to order my foot steps to my next office.'

I walked straight in and the Banking Hall was very busy. I was approached by a woman who was not wearing a uniform; however she had her badge on her. She asked if I could wait as someone would attend to me shortly. I then told her I did not bank with her Bank; I had a question; if Halifax had any positions going. She looked at me upside down. Then she said to "If I give you an application form you complete and bring it back to me; maybe I could do a quick interview on you; would you want to do this?" I replied "Yes please".

She went to the back office a brought a big thick form and a Halifax pen. Well it was very clear that I was not alone; God and his angels were with me. I thank the polite lady and promised to be back with the completed forms. As planned a few moments ago I went next door. I joined the queue, to buy my lunch and tea. The first thing I did when I set down was to thank God for the first two interviews; also thanked him for being with me throughout the day; also for my position I had at the Thistle. Despite what I thought about myself; regarding working in a Bank; I told him he knew what was best for me and I trusted him; therefore I was ready for a change. I asked him to help me complete the forms. It took me 45 minutes to complete the forms and sign the forms.

I went back next door (Halifax Bank) requested to see the polite lady. When she saw me her eyes lit up. She said "Oh; you are back" "Yes" I replied. She took me to the back office where there was a board room. There was another lady there waiting on; first thing she said to me was that; something strange had happened; i.e.

the next person she was to interview had called to cancel. So instead of giving me a quick interview could she give me full interview. The answer was a simple yes from me; this interview was to take 45 minutes; but it went on over an hour. At the end of the day I got the position. I had to call my last interview company I was to attend and cancelled it.

It was clear that Bank had a proper career path for me. The rest is history as I have been working for the same Bank for the last eleven years. Through my employer I have been trained and qualified as a senior banking advisor. So much has happened with my career and there is still much more to come.

We had to ensure the children had good schools. As a result of this we bought a house in Kent; where the good schools are. This alone was a miracle for us. We are so happy we did so as this led to our children moving on to

Universities to pursue their education. So the last eleven years we have seen our children graduate from Universities (Canterbury University & Portsmouth University). We have seen them doing things leaps and bounds with their chosen careers. Now the youngest is still in Secondary school.

Sadly ten years after having been reunited with my children. We lost our daughter in a car accident; two days after she died we received a letter from Thames Valley University stating that she had an unconditional offer to enter University. Our hearts were torn apart as a family. I did not understand how this could be. All I had was ten years with my angel. **Read my next book to know how Against All Odds. we survived even the grief....**

'Her smile would brighten a whole room'

THE family of a young Dartford woman killed in a car crash have paid tribute to their 'beautiful' daughter and sister, Patience Ncube, also known as Patience Jackson. The tragic incident also claimed the lives of two friends.

■ Full story, page

Epilogue

Remember I made a promised in the telephone box (when I became suicidal), to the man upstairs as I called him back then. I promised that if he turned my life around and told me what my purpose or assignment on this earth, I promised that I was going to fulfil my destiny. I would do whatever it takes to achieve this goal. Hence you are reading my book, "Against All Odds I survived", I am true living testimony that there is a God, who sent his son Jesus to die for you and I.

You are not a mistake, you were created for a purpose, and there is an expected end for you. Life might have thrown all kinds of challenges; remember your setbacks or failures in life are not an end, you have the power to disallow every contrary situation in your life, you also have power, will and ability to choose life today, you have been given a free will to choose life. My findings

however is that you cannot do this alone. With God's help, you will overcome. For more information on how to find help, please visit my website: www.fikelephijackson.com you can also email me on: Fikelephi@fikelephijackson.com, follow me on: Facebook www.facebook.com/fikelephijackson Twitter https://twitter.com/Fike8919

I thought I had been rejected, but now I was accepted. I thought I was unlovable, but I found out that He loves me unconditionally. Most importantly, He has a plan and purpose for my life.

Regardless of your faith, beliefs or religion this book is meant for you too. You can find strength to overcome, in my case God found me, he rescued me, redeemed me, and he restored my life. My faith in God has brought me this far. I still pinch myself, and thank God everyday that I am still alive, I have an opportunity to reach out to others and help, mentor, motivate, inspire you and many more. Thank you for reading my book.

Read my next book and learn how I overcome grief of losing my beautiful daughter at such a tender age.